FUNNILY ENOUGH

FUNNILY ENOUGH

JOHN D. SHERIDAN

Illustrated by Paul Noonan

THE TALBOT PRESS LIMITED
EIGHTY-NINE TALBOT STREET, DUBLIN

First Published 1956

Made in the Republic of Ireland, at the Talbot Press Ltd., Dublin

To the Little Man of the cartoons—
that astute and unregarded diplomat
who is society's flywheel, and who,
going from crisis to crisis, lives the
full life in the shade of the
aspidistra.

ACKNOWLEDGMENTS

My best thanks are due once again to the Editor of the *Irish Independent* for permission to use and freely adapt so much material originally published by him ; and also to the Editor of *Books on Trial* (Chicago) for permission to adapt one essay which appeared originally in that journal.

CONTENTS

THE LITTLEST ONE

THE Littlest One wakens at sparrow-chirp, or before it, and occupies herself in various ways until the world is well aired. She dresses her dolls and tells herself stories (I have all this from her own lips), and she goes down to the kitchen several times to keep herself from dying of starvation. These excursions, however, do not affect her prepositional status. She may be down, but as yet she is not officially up. Her attitude to getting up is something like that of Paddy Eamuinn, who on one occasion, when he had been talking to Ned the Post for ten minutes over the half-door, finished the conversation by saying " I think I'll go in and rise."

A century or so later, tiring of her monastic seclusion, the Littlest One goes in next door to remind her parents of the duties of their station in life, and announces to each of them in turn (or rather to the still and death-like shapes beneath the bedclothes—for a parent on these occasions takes evasive action and burrows deep) that unless they bestir themselves she will be late. But she doesn't say " late ". She says " dead late ", and she makes it sound like a passing bell.

And there is no use in trying to reassure her by surfacing and pointing to the clock. For she doesn't trust clocks when the great fear is on her. She regards clocks and parents as partners in a conspiracy for her undoing. She was " late " hours ago, and now she is " dead late ". She has heard all manner of bells and whistles during her eternity of wakefulness, and nothing will comfort her now.

Eventually she decides that since her parents are deaf to the entreaties of their own flesh and blood she might as well make the best of things, so she goes back to bed. But she doesn't go back to her own bed—she gets into the nearest bed, bringing with her a cohort of dolls and Teddy Bears and an assortment of story books. Then, fortified against the possibilities of boredom, she continues her intermittent reveille, tries to get the sleeping beauties interested in her stories, and reminds them with the tenacity of a minute gun that she, their Littlest One, is dead late. And all this puts a great strain on the affection of parents. First it gets them down and then it gets them up, whereupon the Littlest One, following the lead of Paddy Eamuinn, goes back to her own room to rise.

But one day recently the Littlest One found me awake : the thunder had forestalled her. And it was no ordinary thunder—for I am proof against ordinary thunder. It was the kind of thunder-storm that comes once or twice in a decade, the kind of thunder-storm which Paddy Eamuinn says is as good as a mission. Great sheets of corrugated tin were being rattled in the heavens, and the mountains were clearing their throats and getting ready to bite. In the intervals between the shattering peals you could almost hear the lightning sizzling.

The conventional procedure on occasions like this, I believe, is to snuggle under the blankets and pretend that you aren't there—which to me seems both foolish and disrespectful. I don't believe in daring the elements or in playing hide-and-seek with forked instancy. I have my own way of dealing with lightning : I say my prayers, and then I sit up and calculate the odds against being hit. So on this particular morning the Littlest One found me bolt upright and watching the swordplay.

For once she didn't say anything about being dead late. She said : " Do you hear the thunder ? " (She can be as stupid as an adult sometimes. One of these days she will grow up completely and say : " Are you not gone out yet ? ") She herself, it appeared, had been listening to the thunder for quite a long time. She thought it was wonderful. She thought, in fact, that it was " smashing ". But there wasn't much fun in listening to it alone. She needed company. So she climbed into the bed and joined me in the first row of the balcony.

She wasn't frightened; at least, not very much. Lightning could kill you, but thunder couldn't—sure it couldn't ? Thunder was *wizard*.

After a few more desultory commonplaces she made a remark that seemed very remarkable to me, but was not at all remarkable for a lady of her age. " I didn't know at first that it was thunder," she said. " I thought it was only a jet plane."

I like that " only ". I commend it to the back-room boys who are planning to-morrow's marvels. Let them put it in their pipes and smoke it. They may amaze us, but they can't amaze our children, who have already been to the moon in fishbowl helmets. The new atomic planes may scare grandmothers, but the lollipop-suckers will take them for granted.

This comment of the Littlest One linked up later with something that had been lying for a long time in the " Unclassified " section of my mind, and at last I knew where to file it. It was an incident that occurred once at a Military Tattoo. After we had had our fill of whippet tanks and long-snouted guns and lumbering land war-ships, a troop of cavalry in period uniform cantered into the arena, and they didn't look either fierce or convincing. They looked just what they were—soldiers in fancy dress. But a little boy just behind me thought differently. He had not been at all impressed by the mechanical wonders, but when the cavalry appeared he shouted excitedly " Are they *real* horses, mummy ? " For him, the good wine had been kept to the last.

The commonplace is what you are used to, and it is we and not our children who have a distorted sense of values. We, unlike them, lived through the transition stage of modern times. We saw the coming of the motor car, we watched the aeroplane spread its wings, we were there at the birth of wireless. And we are still rubbing our eyes, still taking ourselves—and our times—

far too seriously. Our children were luckier. They answered the telephone as soon as they were big enough to reach it, they think no more of television than of bottled milk, they were reared on talking pictures. So their hierarchy of values is utterly sound, and the Littlest One went right to the heart of things when she said : " I didn't know at first that it was thunder—I thought it was only a jet plane."

The twentieth century may have addled me a little, but it hasn't addled the Littlest One. She is not impressed by the back-room boys. She has her own way of assessing wonders. She puts tadpoles before television, and thunder before thunder-jets. Her instinctive religious sense is not crusted over, as ours is, with self-importance, and she knows modern alchemy for the sorry thing that it is. She is a child of her age, but her heart is in the right place. When she is on the beach at Portmarnock she may look up once in a while to tell me the make of a passing aeroplane, or pause to give me some details of the latest in atomic submarines, but she is not half as interested in these tiny things as I am, and when she has set me right and enlightened my ignorance she gives her whole mind to the tremendous problem of making a sand castle that will come out of the bucket as smooth and unbroken as an Egyptian fez.

THE CAROL-SINGERS

WE had our first carol-singers the other night, although it is a good three weeks before Christmas, and from now on there will be no rest for a man with small change in his pocket—unless he is strong-minded enough to ignore knocks, or patient enough to sit in darkness and so avoid them altogether. I am not against carol-singers, but I think that nowadays they come too early and too often. When I was young, carol-singers were sudden and seldom—like snow, or a piper's band. They waited until the very brink of the feast, and were not far in front of the herald angels. They worked on a short tether, too, and never ventured outside their own parish, but nowadays carol-singers map out fresh districts like burglars, so that you may have to pay hush-money to several contingents on the same night.

On this subject, as on so many others, the Littlest One doesn't agree with me. She thinks that the carol-singers couldn't come too early or too often, that they should begin immediately after Hallow Eve and keep whacking away till Little Christmas. For the past fortnight she has been putting a tiny addendum to her night prayers, and it comes as soon as she rises off her knees—showing that her mind cannot be wholly on her orisons. She says "I hope the carol-singers will come to-night," and sometimes she adds: "Hadn't we a fire in the chimney once when I was small ? " If she could have the fire brigade and the carol-singers on the same night her cup would be full.

She likes the carol-singers because they have a licence to do all the things that a respectable young lady, once abed, would like to do but daren't—to knock at all the doors, and waken all the babies, and frighten all the birds. She wants the night to be filled with music, and so, at this time of year, she lies awake listening and is as intent as a rabbit at the mouth of his burrow. She may be deceived, though never for long, by barking dogs or singing errand boys, but she knows her own when they come, and after that there is no danger of falling asleep.

The real beauty of carol-singing from her point of view is that it overlaps in each direction. It works up to a slow crescendo, holds its climax for fully five minutes, and then fades slowly in the distance until the far-away door-knockings could be overlain by the scratching of a mouse behind the wardrobe. It is not a fierce and short-lived joy, like a passing fire-engine : it lasts as long as a slab of sticky toffee. It gives the tumultuous, agitated heart time to settle down again, and when the last knock comes fairy-faint from the farthest house in all the world, the Littlest One is soothed and ready for sleep.

I was not as lucky as the Littlest One when I was young, for I slept three storeys up (we had a funny house—it had three storeys at the back and only two in front), far from the rattle of pots in the kitchen and the stories and laughs of " the room ". Even the noise of footsteps was denied me, for the footsteps were at the front of the house and I was at the back. At spaced intervals I could hear the whine of the trams as they climbed up to Whitehall and the very rim of the city, but there was poor comfort in it; it made me think of wolves, and banshees, and children done to death in the forest. I lay there miserably at the top of the house with only the silence for company.

And unless my memory plays me false, there was less carol-singing in those days than there is now. Indeed I don't remember any at all. But I do remember the thud of bombs and the rattle of machine guns, and perhaps that is the explanation. " The Trouble " put a veto on a lot of things, and carol-singing may have been one of them.

But in these latter years I am making up for this early poverty. I am getting my fill of carol-singers, and while I am waiting for the knock I lose my place and my thoughts slip out of gear. I am prepared to contribute to anything in reason, but my motives are dead wrong. The money I give to the carol-singers is no better than blackmail; I want to get it over quickly and get back to my typing; I pay the piper but I never listen to the tune.

All of which shows that I am badly in need of carol-singing. I think of it not as a blessing and a recall, but as an interruption—which shows that I have grown used to my prison cell and am out of touch with freedom. I am like a convict who grumbles because a thrush lights on his window-sill and distracts him from his reading; and if I were half the man I should be I would drop everything and listen.

A

I still regard carol-singing as an interruption, and so I am still in heresy: and the heresy is the one that Christmas comes to crush—the heresy that things are what they seem. When you grudge the time and the money that are spent on Christmas you are in a bad way; and when you regard it as a moment of sentimental folly, instead of as a moment of hard-headed sanity, you are due for a scouring.

The Littlest One, of course, has no need of any such re-orientation. Her sense of values has never gone awry, and she is still on the side of Christmas. She hears the carol-singers before I do, because her ears are attuned, whereas I have let deafness creep upon me unawares.

But it is not necessarily a permanent disability, and since I have a bigoted resident tutor there is every reason for hope. I can even detect a slight improvement already. I still think of the carol-singers as a nuisance, but I am coming to think of them as a salutary nuisance. I still think that they come a little too early, but I am beginning to realize that they may be working to an old and reliable time-table that I seem to have mislaid. And in a little while, if my progress continues, I shall remember that Christmas is not a day but a season, that the season works up to one intense moment which may be called a climax, and is much more than an economic climax, and that Advent comes when it does for the simple reason that it takes the best part of a month to get us into spiritual trim.

The position, therefore, is not by any means hopeless, and I think that the Littlest One—and the carol-singers —will have me right before the herald angels sing.

B

A HAPPY CHRISTMAS

(with apologies to Ogden Nash)

On all sides I am admonished to do my shopping early,
And so avoid the hurly-burly,
And also enable home-for-Christmas shop assistants to
    get away from the fuss in time to catch the last bus.
No one is more conscious than I am of the merits of
    the new dispensation, but nevertheless I regard it with
    a total absence of elation:
Which is very reactionary and non-co-operative of me,
    I fear,
But then I am a very reactionary and non-co-operative
    fellow at this time of year.
I want to have my old-fashioned Christmas fun and to
    do all the things that in the best circles are no longer
    done.
I want to be trampled and squeezed to death, to dig
    with and be dug by elbows while I struggle for breath,
To move in a sardine-crush of last-minute reactionary
    fellow-shoppers in places like the Coombe and Henry
    Street,
Where I have to ask total strangers not to loiter on my
    feet.
I want to be one of the gawkers who stand and look at
    the hawkers,
To be importuned to contribute to the gaiety of nations
    by buying a dancing sailor or a Christmas motto or
    the last—the very last—of the Christmas decorations.

And I see clearly when I am swirling in this vast
    Dickensian sea,
That although there are plenty of early-shopping, get-
    it-over-quickly people in the city there is also a fair
    sprinkling of obscurantist fellows like me.

.   .   .   .   .

The Post Office, in order to save itself trouble, goes to
    a lot of trouble asking me to post early.
And so I do—well, fairly.
I have improved considerably in this respect, but I shall
    never be one of the elect.
Most of my friends, however, have come to heel and
    send their cards as early as anyone could wish,
Which is high-minded and premature and conformist,
    but not quite my dish,
For I don't see why the literary side of Christmas should
    be over and done before the thing has properly begun.
And all this week, previous and untimely snow-and-
    stagecoach cards have come slobbering through my
    letter-box and into my hall,
Where my innocent children, knowing no better, fight
    for them when they fall,
While I sit in the kitchen chewing the fat of my bacon,
And thinking that in a year or two my Christmas cards
    will be waiting for me when I come back from my
    summer vacation.
What I would like now is one—even one—Christmas
    letter, and I don't care what sort of a card is in it,
Provided that it comes at the very last minute—
One here-I-am-and-don't-be-hard-on-me letter that
    gets a reprieve

From the hard-working folk in the General Sorting
    Office and is sent out as a charity with the last of
    the late postmen on Christmas Eve.

Another thing I want at Christmas is a drunk man—
Not really drunk—God forbid!—but full enough to
    make some kind of a fuss,
And wish "A Happy Christmas" to everyone in the
    bus.
I want him jolly,
And for preference he should be insecurely attached to
    a white and bruised turkey and a lump of holly.
I also want him to be festooned with parcels that he
    drops and keeps picking up again until all the paper's
    busted,
And every time he picks them up he must raise his hat
    to the grim-looking warship of a woman in the corner
    seat who will have nothing to do with him and who
    is obviously disgusted.

.   .   .   .

I can stand most greetings at Christmas but I can't
    stand "The compliments of the season"—
Which is a heretical twisting of a blessing and is not
    even an abbreviated prayer :
If you can't rise to a better salutation than this you
    should just leave it there.
And if you are too liberal and progressive to use holy
    and Christian words this blessed night
I can only apologise, and pray for you, and explain that
    I took you for a traditional European in the half-light.

I may be common and vulgar in wanting crowds and
    fuss at Christmas time, and a certain amount of din,
But I seem to remember hearing that there were crowds
    in Bethlehem, and no room at the inn.
There was quiet and peace on the hillside, and in the
    cave,
But it was the noisy multitude that He came to save.

Having got a lot off my chest now I must be going,
    for I want to get a dancing crocodile and a mechanical
    mouse and some of the long decorations,
And a few last-minute presents and cards for my friends
    and relations;

But before I go let me wish a Happy and a Holy
    Christmas to all in Corglass and Ballydehob and
    Belleek,
Not excepting even those misguided folk who sent
    me premature Christmas cards in the beginning of
    last week.

> I send my salutations
> Without any reservations.
> *May Mary and her Son*
> *Bless us every one.*

ON KNEES

WHEN I look at the little knees of this house—which are as scarred and pitted as the face of the moon, but much blacker—I wonder how so many of us adults have managed to grow up reasonably intact. For the way of a young knee is hard, and the odds are heavily against survival. It is rasped against pebble-dashed walls, shot through with pellets of grit, bruised on rough concrete, and blooded on broken glass; and when its coat of dirt is removed it is revealed as a jagged pattern of old and new hurts, a mass of healing and bealing.

A boy will sometimes surrender a wounded knee, but seldom for long and never willingly. You get the towel, the basin, the bandages, and the disinfectant, but you don't get the knee—except for brief uneasy tenancies during which it is still a moving target, so that when the owner forecloses on the lease he gets his property back with its mineral rights practically intact.

You give him a lecture on blood-poisoning then, and he seems to be enjoying it. But what he is really enjoying is the respite. He is quite prepared to die in agony, provided that the agony is post-dated; he is ready to lose a leg later on, so long as you allow him full use of it now; and since nothing short of an anaesthetic will get it from him you have no option but to agree.

He may lend you the leg, apprehensively, for a second or two, but he will jerk it back convulsively at the first touch of the swab, and after several false starts the operation has to be abandoned for want of a patient. And the strange thing is that the leg comes to no harm. It should mortify and fall off, or at least turn blue enough for the surgeon's knife, but instead it blooms and stays on. If the nasty rod-like shapes that come to life under the microscope are half as dangerous as their Latin names seem to suggest, then there must be some congenital immunity in a boy's knee that fortifies him against sepsis—otherwise full-grown adults would be much scarcer than they are, and one-legged ones more common.

The miracle of the human knee is that combination of rigidity and flexibility which adapts it to the needs of navvies and ballerinas and makes it as useful to the professional footballer as to the higher executive officer. Nothing less than the blow of a sledge will shatter it, yet it is the most delicate of hinges, an equipoise of sheer mechanical perfection, a fool-proof component that is serviced once and for all when it leaves the factory. It is self-oiling, self-adjusting, and—in normal conditions—guaranteed for ever. It braces itself against one stress and relaxes to take another. It is the first line of the body's defences to go into action, and the last to yield. There may be a glimmer of hope when a man is beaten to the ropes, but there is no hope when he is beaten to his knees—there is nothing left to him then but to sue for peace and get what terms he can.

The human knee is such a magnificent and versatile member that all other knees seem caricatures by comparison. In this matter of knees the frog and the ape are no better served than the ostrich and the hen. Man alone of all the animals knows the full secret and purpose of knees, for he can do one thing with them that none of the brutes can do : the camel and the elephant can give clumsy imitations, but man alone can kneel properly and without losing dignity—the best that the others can do is to use their knees as half-way halts in the laborious process of lying down.

To the child, his mother's knee is his first nursery and headquarters, and he comes back to it again and again to ease his hurts and tell his troubles and get little refresher courses in self-confidence. Orphanages are wonderful places, and much heroic work is done in them, but they are woefully short of mothers' knees, and modern psychology is a sorry substitute. The father's knee has less hallowed associations than the mother's, but it, too, has its place in the educative process and it may not be spared without spoiling the child. It is at our mother's knee, and across our father's, that we learn our first and best lessons, and everyone who has been properly brought up is an ex-pupil of the patella.

If man is the only animal that can kneel properly and with dignity it is not because he is better adapted physically for this position than the other animals, but rather because he is the only animal that can give the act purpose and significance, and accept the discomfort of a position that is somewhat unnatural from a motive that is clearly supernatural. The brute beast fulfils its end and gives glory by doing brutish and instinctive things. It can give praise and thanks by spreading its wings, or climbing trees, or nosing in the mud of rivers, or trumpeting in the forest. All that is asked of it is to give a service which it cannot withhold, so that its full ordained perfection is to scratch for worms, or crack nuts, or raise curled whorls on wet beaches. It does what it must do, and is incapable of doing more or less. Its poverty is that it cannot add or subtract a tithe of worship. But there is one animal of whom more is expected, one animal that can give or withhold, bless or curse, adore or blaspheme, one animal that must sink down to rise up—and every time he goes on his knees he bumps his head against the stars.

NEW YEARS LONG AGO

ON New Year's Eves, long, long ago, we kept guard between us, dozing off at intervals when sleep got the better of excitement, and waking a dozen times in panic to the horrible thought that we had slept right through the tumult and the clangour. But there was no real likelihood of so terrible a treason. The flesh was weak, but our strength lay in numbers. There were nine of us, and we never missed the bells. Every time a sleeper awoke he would make a tour of the other bed-rooms and be sure of finding at least one sentry wide-awake. Our bouts of wakefulness overlapped, and between us we kept a watch on the night.

When it came first it was a dim, far-away sound; like the horns of Elfland faintly blowing. We strained our ears as we knelt at the open window (we always kept it at pneumonia level on New Year's Eve) and rested the elbows of our nightshirts on the sills. And then, one by one, all the bells joined in, and the whole world was awake.

We lived in what was then the most northerly suburb of the city (how it has grown in the meantime!) and the nearest chiming steeple was a good mile-and-a-half away, so that the sound of the New Year's bells came to us in a distorted jumble. Late starters overtook others on the way—perhaps they caught a faster breeze—and spoiled the melodic line, so that the whole thing seemed arbitrary and without plan. It was as if each separate bell had broken loose and gone into business for itself—and that was just how we wanted it.

Every now and then, factory whistles would scream up and out in lawless outcroppings that made the whole sky tingle, and round the base of each of these towers of sound the peals of the bells fluttered like garlands. And from the boats in the river (I suppose no one welcomes the New Year more willingly than a seaman away from home) came the growling of the sirens—a hoarse, tremulous bass that gave body and substance to the whole symphony.

We shivered as we knelt at the open windows, and with delight as well as with cold, for our spines were tuning forks, and we responded physically to every change in the wild tumult.

Then, little by little, the city grew quiet again. The steeples dropped out in their turn, like spent runners; the factory whistles trailed off in splintery echoes. But even then there was something to listen for: one of the river boats might give an extra toot or two for good measure, a bellringer might lean on his rope for joy, a factory whistle might start again on a short breath—like an enthusiast trying to work up another round of applause.

But at last it was all over, and there was no sound then but the sound of the wind and the creak of the floor-boards. Down in the heart of the city the revellers were still singing with linked hands, but that was far, far away, and we knew nothing about it. For us, the old year was out and the new year was in : and we felt lonely, and cold, and happy, all at once.

We crept back into bed then and pulled the blankets over our heads, and we stayed in our dark caverns until the heat of our own breaths took the shivers out of us. But we didn't go to sleep. It would have been sacrilege to go to sleep, for the most magical part of the most magical night was still to come. There was something else to wait for—something that I lay awake and listened for every New Year's Eve between pram and long trousers. Sometimes I fancy I can hear it still on New Years' Eves. Sometimes I find myself listening with the ear of childhood for a voice that will never come again.

It was the voice of a great friend of ours who lived further up the road. He was a fine fellow. Indeed he was more than a fine fellow, for he was a fine fellow " although "—and the " although " covered the fact that he was " of a different way of thinking ". Every New Year's Eve he went to a church service around midnight, and though we wondered what sort of a service could be held at midnight, and fancied that it must be very, very black, we gave it a qualified pardon because our good friend went to it; and also because, on his way home, he stopped to wish us a Happy New Year. Ours wasn't his first call, and it was always very late when he came, but he never forgot us. And he always wished us a *Happy* New Year, I am glad to say; not a *Bright* New Year (whatever that may be), or, worse still, a Bright and Prosperous New Year. He was too much of a Christian for that, and although he wasn't " our way of thinking " he had his theology right.

We liked the wish and the blessing, but what we liked even more was the way in which it was given, for he always shouted it through the letter-box. He might easily have been charged with being a public nuisance, and with creating a disturbance in the small hours, but he took this risk willingly and never disappointed us. When the bells were done and the night was still he would tip-toe up to our hall door and bellow the " Happy New Year " that we were all waiting for. It was a great Christian shout that rattled all the bedroom doors on its way up to flatten itself against the fanlight in the attic.

Waiting for it was a delight and a torture. No one could keep guard for the rest now, for it would be all over and done with in the space of a sneeze. There was no compromise with sleep, no dozing off. The price of the blessing was eternal vigilance. We scarcely dared to breathe. We lay there in the darkness—lay for hours, it seemed—waiting for that glad neighbourly blessing, waiting for our Happy New Year.

And it always came.   It always came until it stopped for ever.

I remember the first New Year's Eve that he missed. The bells had an eerie sound that night.   They were like a requiem.   The sirens from the river caught at our hearts, and the last wisps of the factory whistles left us in a world that was cold, and lonely, and unutterably sad.

And afterwards, we lay there miserably in the darkness, huddled together under the blankets, and listening in spite of ourselves : listening for the quiet footfall and the faint rattle of the letter-box.   It did rattle once, very late in the night, and we held our breath in panic, but no glad shout followed it, and the whole world was still.

THE OLDEST COW

WHEN the headlines are full of headaches I turn for comfort to the small print; and it was there that I found this delightful news item that I have kept in my heart ever since. There it was, tucked away inconspicuously, and published, no doubt, not for its own sweet sake, but because some rummaging sub-editor saw at a glance that it would fill a space that needed filling. Here it is in all its glory :—

> A cow in Haverfordwest, Pembrokeshire, is believed to be the oldest in the world. She is thirty-five. Her sight and hearing are excellent, but she has a touch of rheumatism.

There may be older cows in Darjeeling, Wagga Wagga, or New Haven (Conn.), and I should not be surprised to find an objection lodged from Upper Tirladen, but that is neither here nor there : what matters is that there is an old, old cow in Haverfordwest, Pembroke-shire, and that her sight and hearing are still excellent. And I am not surprised to learn that she has a touch of rheumatism—she probably got it from lying on damp grass.

One advantage of being a very old man, as compared with being a very old cow, is that you can boast about your age. You can waggle your few stumps of teeth— or gnash your State dentures—and say : " Aye, dang me, ninety-nine I be come Whitsun, and never a day sick in me life. Never did hold much with doctors and such new-fangled stuff." To an old man, every new dawn is an achievement, and the deaths of his contempo-raries gives him fresh courage. For the old take a malevolent delight in outliving their competitors, and although when they talk to the reporters they usually ascribe their longevity to whiskey, wearing red flannel next the skin, or not taking hot baths, they really regard it in the same light as a victory at backgammon or shove-ha'penny—as the reward of skill and intelligence. I like the story of the ancient backwoodsman who, when the revivalist minister asked him " How come, Ephraim, that you hate nobody ? " replied " The ———— is all dead."

But an old cow is denied simple pleasures like these, for she keeps no tally of the years and the abstraction of age is beyond her. No doubt visitors to Haverford-west, when they have seen the cracked belfry, and the fourteenth-century almshouse, and the castle moat, are taken to see the oldest cow. But the satisfaction is one-sided, for the celebrity doesn't know that she is a cele-

c

brity. There may be some fun in being an old cow, but there is no fun at all in being the oldest cow.

The old lady's sight and hearing may be excellent, but again she doesn't know. If her hearing failed completely she would have no regrets, and if blindness came in the night she would spend the rest of her life waiting patiently for the dawn. For that matter, a trickle of eyesight would serve her wants now. All she needs is to be able to see her way round the doorpost of the byre and through the slap into the Long Meadow; and if the whitethorn hedge were no more than a blur she would not long for the days when she could see the shawls of mist on the shoulders of the hills.

With us, eyesight fails gradually, and its deterioration is marked by heartbreak stages. We screw our eyes at the telephone directory until the figures baffle us completely, and we do without glasses until we can no longer see the mustard on the side of the plate or tell the fat from the lean. But the cow gets no warnings like these. All she has to do at feeding time is to put down her head and munch away. God has put her dinner where she can get at it easily, and when her eyes fail her she still has a nose to lead her to the sweetest clover.

The old lady in Haverfordwest still has sharp hearing, but she could do with a deal less. The days of alarms are long past, and there is no panic now to make her hoist her tail and thunder off like a buffalo. She can still hear the song of the lark and the rattle of the carts in the lane, but if she couldn't she would neither miss them nor remember : she would be equipped for full living if she were as deaf as a post.

God is very good to old cows, for they grow old unknown to themselves, and they approach the end without realizing that there is an end. They have no fear of death, no numbing premonitions. They cling to life, but when their time comes they go quietly and without fuss. There is no fearsome gap between the known and the unknown. It is they, and not we, who " fall asleep ", and they have no need of the comfort of the last and most futile of euphemisms.

Their way of life is fixed and constant, and there is no disharmony in their nature—as there is in ours. There is wisdom hidden in the tag " the tune the old cow died of ", for the last beat is the last beat, and after that there is nothing at all.

I like to think of this old cow in Haverfordwest, Pembrokeshire. She may not be the oldest cow in the world, but she is old enough for me, and I keep her in my heart as an antidote against a world that is full of tumult and disquiet. Every time I open my morning paper and go from crisis to crisis I think of a green meadow in Haverfordwest and take solace in the thought of this old cow, munching away quietly, trustingly, living in the eternal present and adding each slice of the future to it as it comes. I rejoice in the thought of her continuing health and happiness, and am glad that she has so little to bother her. And she need not worry unduly about her touch of rheumatism—for this, considering her way of life, is a normal occupational hazard.

ROOKS IN THE HIGH TREES

I LOOKED up at the nurseries of the rooks—the first skyscrapers, surely—and thought of the boys of long ago who put wads of cotton-wool into shaving-soap tins and climbed to the very eaves of the sky to gather rook eggs. Up and up they went until the man-thick branches thinned down to whiplash, sky-fingering besoms, and at every foot of the way the fighter planes of the rooks cried havoc about their heads. It was brazen, villainous work, and it called for the brave foolishness of youth. Even if your courage gave out before you reached the nests (and mine always did) you felt that you had risked something and gained something, and you swaggered a little when you came down. What fine fellows we all were before sense and cowardice came to us together.

The rook nests, when I looked up at them the other day, were like tangles in untidy hair. There was a fortuitous look about them—as if the twigs had dropped in clotted lumps and lodged in the forks of themselves. Something was afoot, for there is always a crisis in a gathering of rooks, and the whole colony was in a ferment. The litigants dipped and wheeled in cumbrous flight, and flapped their lawyers' gowns in endless disputation about titles and party branches. Rooks are noisy builders. Everything they do is done to the hoarse razor-squawk of man-and-wife wrangling. But they know their trade, and the crazy things they fashion ride the gale.

When darkness had put a necklace of lights about the throat of the bay, a boisterous wind came up from the sea and strengthened into urgent gusts that fretted the trees, and rattled the window panes, and set up intermittent ghostly creakings behind the bedroom skirtings. I lay awake and listened to it all. The wind was like a river in the trees, and I thought of the thick branches swaying like masts and the high twigs fighting for breath.

And I thought, too, of the rooks in their nurseries. Once or twice I heard mutterings from them, but there was no panic. It was the sleepy chattering of folk who knew that their house was proof against disaster, the boasting of builders who had inherited the secrets of stresses. And sometimes I heard a single watery cry— as if a watchman rook was calling the hour and telling the citizens that all was well.

It was not a wild night, as nights go, but a frolic wind played itself. It tumbled milk bottles on doorsteps and set bin lids clanging on pavements. It tugged at all untethered things, and carried off what it could. But though it combed and clawed at the trees, the tangled nests stood firm. They were still there in the morning, when the rooks came out to yawn and preen themselves. Not a slate was out of place in their high city.

I have never seen a rook's nest at close range, but I have looked into linnets' nests, and blackbirds' nests, and wrens' nests—like goose eggs wrapped in moss, if I remember rightly. And I know that each bird works from its family blueprint and follows an unlearned pattern of behaviour. Some are weavers, some are plasterers, some are milliners, and some are all three.

As a general rule, too, the smaller the bird the better the nest. The eagle is far above comfort, but the robin is houseproud and lives snug.

Most of the other birds weave feathers for upholstery, or smooth out mud floors with their trowel beaks, but the rook is not interested in furniture, smoothness, or interior decoration. He is an engineer, pure and simple. He chooses an impossible site and then lays girder on girder. His job is to build, and the little skills of finch and sparrow pale beside his rough genius. These others make miniatures in sheltered places and boast about their eiderdowns : he works in the mass and under the open sky, and he lays his foundations in the teeth of the gale.

We sometimes look down on rooks because they have neither voice nor grace of movement, because they are contentious by nature and argue all day long outside their untidy tenements. And undoubtedly, by our standards, there is something clownish and awkward about them. They have a touch of vulgarity, and they set no value on privacy, or quietness, or reticence. They are raucous, thieving, and audacious. They walk splay-footed among our seedlings, and they make a great killing when the radishes are young. They take a living where they find it, and ask no man's leave.

We see no good in the rook, and he, in his turn, treats us with something like contempt. He harries the growing crops, but he keeps his distance and asks no favours. He is as independent as a pirate or a gipsy, and he has the courage of his vices. He never fraternises, never says grace. He comes openly to rob, and you can like it or lump it.

But I cannot help wondering at times whether this dour and uncompromising independence is authentic, and whether rooks really are the rebels that they seem to be. We give them little tolerance—we have even named a rifle and a pie after them—but they have a fondness for our paddocks and live much nearer our chimneys than they need. They are born brigands, and they take a sore toll of our grain and turnips, but between raids they withdraw only to the outskirts of the citadel, and their real longing may be, not so much to be close to the farm as to be close to the farmer. They build high, as if they wanted to get as far away from us as possible, but the trees are only half-a-furlong from the hall door. Rooks are always out of reach, but seldom out of sight. They are never very far away—as the crow flies.

LINE OF WASHING

A LINE of washing is not only a wind-gauge and a barometer but a head-count and a means test, for the whole family hangs from it and nothing is hid. This is why tramps and pedlars, before they knock at the front door, usually make a short reconnaissance at the back.

Travelling women, too, have their own way of studying the position before they attack. If the clothes-line is obviously His-and-Hers, and all the swinging effigies are adult size, the experienced travelling woman says: " God bless you, mam, may you never know want, and would you happen to have such a thing about the place as an old suit that himself wouldn't be needing ? " But if the line is chock-a-block with tiny flutterings hanging three from a peg she knows that " himself " is wearing an old suit and wondering where its successor is to come from; and so she says: " God bless you, mam, and your houseful of lovely children, and would you have such a thing as a pair of babby shoes that would suit the child here ? "

For a house with children can be picked out three gardens away: it will have not only a main clothes-line but several branch lines, and the ragged overflow will be hung discreetly on the bushes. And if there is a baby in the house the thing is easier still. An adult house can space its washings and choose its wash-days, but a baby house is always in hot water and it washes

its clothes as often as it washes its table-gear. His
Majesty's pennants blow in every breeze, and his stern-
flag is never struck.

" Everything comes out in the wash " is only a half-
truth, for the rest comes out in the wash-basket. The
clothes-line is the real informer. It keeps nothing back.
It turns private affairs into public audits, and makes
every sheet a balance sheet. A shirt on a clothes-line
cannot be hid, even though thereby hangs a tail that
is thrift's handiwork, and there is one day in the week
when every home makes open confession.

In assessing the resources of a house from its showing
on wash-day it must be remembered that there is more
here than meets the eye. Everything must be multiplied
by two at least, for this is multiple-entry bookkeeping,
and the fellows of every visible and declared asset exist
somewhere else in decent seclusion. When you look at
a line of washing you are looking only at the reserves,
for there is a full quota on active service. The first
team is playing away, and only the substitutes are on
view.

And at first they don't look a very promising lot.
They move sluggishly and are obviously in poor training.
They carry too much weight, and they lack sparkle. It
is only when they begin to dry out that they really show
their paces. An arm flaps here, and a leg there. A
pillow-slip jumps up to see what is doing on the line
next door. Lighter garments turn somersaults, and then
find themselves becalmed on the blind side. But even
the heavier pieces, like sheets and blankets, kick enough
to show their petticoats, and every sudden gust sets the

whole line swinging. Once in a while, too, the sup-
porting pole cants over—as if the bathroom towels had
deliberately wheeled the scrum.

A line of washing reveals many secrets, but it also
thins down the number of secrets. It grades us into
age-groups and income-groups, and shows us as unmis-
takably male or female, but it shows also that within
these broad categories we are much of a muchness. The
clothes-peg is the great equaliser, and a touch of soap-
and-water makes the whole world kin. There is nothing
that sets off the managing director's socks from any
other socks, and Julia O'Grady's intimacies might well
belong to the Colonel's lady.

A line of washing has no reticence. It shows us up
for what we are : stuffed men, padded out to a fictitious
bulk and gravity. Like the onion, we come away in
layers. But the clothes that hang from our garden lines
mock not us but themselves. They are not so much
caricatures as scarecrows. Clothes may make the
man, but it is even more true to say that man makes
the clothes, for a disembodied shirt is both pathetic and
ludicrous, and not all the wind in the world can fill an
empty sleeve. We are sorry enough things when we are
peeled, God knows, but our peelings are sorrier still,
and the best salesman in the shop is the dummy
in the window.

No one likes washing clothes, and the dislike goes
deeper far than the work involved. A garment in a
wash-tub is a forlorn thing. It is as hideous as a shroud,
and it has neither character nor significance. It is still

repulsive on the clothes-line, but it is at least a shade nearer the day of redemption. It spurts up into size and shape, as if it were longing for reincarnation, and then subsides into mere potentiality. It can never be filled until we fill it, but when it gets as far as the garden line it is on the way back. And so, the Monday washing lines in the suburbs are like signal pennants reading " Operation Proceeding According to Plan." All is not over, but the worst is over. It is now the turn of wind and sun, and the first mate sits down happily to the best cup of tea of the week.

Civilization may have begun with a roof and a fire, but it came of age with a line of washing, and it was no mere whim that caused the ancient philosopher to take up residence in a tub. Once man learned how to spin and weave, and hankered for something soft to wear next his skin, the rest followed. Clothes were washed in rivers, pounded on stones, and spread to dry on sunny rocks.

In due course came the first clothes-line, and no doubt it was man-made and woman-inspired. What the good wife did not know, however, was that she was being given enough rope to hang herself, and that from that on her sex would be bound and indentured : for the burden of the tub and the clothes-line is Eve's rather than Adam's, except in monasteries, lighthouses, battle-ships, model lodging houses, and certain other places where the sons of freedom live in community.

But the curse of Eden is not shared unjustly, and a man who earns his bread by the sweat of his brow can surely look to his wife to keep him in clean underings. And the old nursery rhyme still applies as a rough description of the division, though it needs to be adapted to modern conditions. It is the wife, not the maid, who is hanging out the clothes, and though the husband is still in the counting-house he is counting someone else's money. New inventions have made life a little easier, no doubt, but it is still a pretty grim business; and the real work of the world is done, not by rollers and tumblers, or by cog wheels and revolving drums, but by washing-machines and totting-machines who have taken each other for better for worse, for richer for poorer.

MEN ONLY

WHEN a woman says " I look a fright " she invariably adds, by way of explanation, " My hair is a show." She is referring, not to a worsening condition due to the ravages of time, but to a temporary set-back due to want of time. She seems to be making a statement, but she is really planning a campaign.

At a time like this, almost everything that she says is marked by undercurrents that the trained male ear can detect at once, and she can put a wealth of pathos into such a simple remark as " I think the fire needs coal." She conveys one idea in dozens of ways, and the idea is that, overworked and downtrodden as she is, she has not been able to give proper attention to what should be a high priority.

Her tone is that of a man writing to the papers to point out that there is woodworm in the timbers of the cathedral or that the damp is ruining one of the finest portraits in the civic gallery. She is not, it would appear, urging a selfish interest. Her point is that a great public shame has come upon us and that the forces of civilization should be mobilized without delay. She champions her own hair, and she does it by getting in everyone else's hair.

If there is only one woman whose hair looks a fright, this is bad : but if there are two, this is good, for then they can make a pact and promise service for service. Amateur hair-waving is carried on in the way harvesting used to be carried on—one for all, and all for one. A night's work earns a night's work, a favour done is a favour due, and sister priestesses collaborate in making one another beautiful—and greater love than this no woman can show.

One of the team sits in a chair with a towel round her neck, and the other stands behind the chair and works on the hair in front of her with pipe cleaners, wads of paper, saucers of evil-smelling liquid, and metal clips, and she moulds it into shapes that were not in the original blueprint. The lady behind the chair has tender, loving hands, but her lips are bitter. (This is because her mouth is full of metal clips.) The lady in the chair looks more of a fright than ever, but a much happier fright. There is a smug " Wait till you see me " look in her eye, and she is borne up by the thought of the glory to come.

The work of restoration is long and tedious, and it calls for a dedicated loyalty and a defective sense of smell; for the smell of the lotion is so revolting that none but the sisterhood could stay in the same room with it, and at times it is hard to stay in the same house with it. The general impression one gets in the other rooms is of being next door to a burning fish-glue factory.

But the amateur hair-do, no matter how successful, can never give a lift to the spirit. It may bring back a woman's curls, but it makes her feel that she is not only downtrodden but married to a failure, and in serious depressions, as well as before weddings and annual dinners, the job has to be done by a professional.

Then it involves long absences from the domestic scene, during which the rice pudding blackens in the oven and one of the children usually breaks an arm. More often than not, too, a man calls with a half-ton of coal and has to bring it away again.

Meanwhile, the truant, recking nothing of these little tragedies, is sitting immobile in her little cell under an immense acorn-shaped helmet. What exactly happens in these perfumed temples no man knows—except, of course, the professional hairdresser, and he won't tell. All that the rest of us know is that straight ways are made crooked and then lapse again, for a " permanent ", despite the time spent on it, is never permanent. It may be a thing of beauty, but it is not a joy for ever. Business people, it seems, have no regard for the niceties of the language and will do anything for profit. A " permanent " is really a temporary, unbreakable china breaks, waterproofs often aren't, and an insurance man will sell you a " comprehensive " policy which covers everything but the things that happen and is not noticeably comprehensive.

We men, as I say, know little of what goes on under the hairdresser's metal helmet, and we are not curious. For our interest in hair is not what it used to be : women's hair is a major industry and a life-long worry, but ours is a vanishing holding that comes out every day under the comb. And, little by little, we cease to worry about it. When his curls go, or when the scalp begins to show through widening pink weals, hair, to a man, is simply the stuff he beds his hat on until his ears take up its support.

This philosophic detachment, however, is not attained overnight. It is the end of a long story. Pride gives way to fear, fear to hope and hair restorers, hope to despair, and despair to resignation; and by the time the hair that is left approximates in colour and texture to the stuff that grows on the chins of coconuts, the subject has invented little fictions for his comforting. He looks in the mirror only from certain angles, trains long hairs across wide stretches of open country, and tells himself that he is going a little thin on the top.

But he never complains, never asks for sympathy, never says " My hair is awful—I look a fright ", for he knows that the situation is bound to deteriorate and that the worst is yet to be. And when at last he can find no comfort at all in the mirror, and is known as "Curly" to the other members of his Sunday fourball, he tells himself that baldness gives a man a touch of character and brings out the strong lines of his face.

ON THE BRIDGE

I SURPRISED myself the other evening by doing something that I haven't done for years—I stood for a while on the bridge, and for no other reason than that there is a river underneath. I stood on the bridge and looked down over the parapet on the brown, opaque water that the city had soiled and muddied. You can always be sure of the river. Sometimes the lion is in the inner cage, and you may pass the Fire Station every day for a month without seeing a brass helmet, but the river is always there.

And on this evening I had it almost to myself. The only other person standing on the bridge was an indomitable and evidently tone-deaf musician who was wringing noises from a jangly and ill-tuned instrument. But the musician wasn't looking at the river—he had his back to it. Like his hurrying clients, he put business before pleasure.

I didn't stay long on the bridge, for loitering on city bridges is a dangerous pastime, unless you have had the foresight to provide yourself with something that will take the bare look off you—a collection of sketches, a mandoline, or a bootblack's stand. You are all right as long as you keep your back to the parapet, but if you look down into the river for any length of time you will be joined by a ghoul who, detaching himself hungrily from the scurrying crowd, looks from you to

47

the river and from the river to you, obviously wondering just where you saw the body.

One man looking over a bridge is bad enough, but two is the makings of a crowd, and before long you will be surrounded by eager citizens who smell a coroner's inquest. Newcomers will turn to you hopefully—since from your position you are clearly a person of long standing and vested interests—and ask " Eh, mister, what's up ? " They are all hoping for the worst, and they see themselves already standing at counters and giving grisly, first-hand accounts larded with " God's truth—I seen it with me own two eyes not half-an-hour ago!"

When it becomes clear that nothing is up, and that there is nothing under the bridge but grey stone and the oily river, things will take an ugly turn, and early arrivals, questioned by people on the outskirts, will nod in your direction and say : " It's your man there—I seen him looking down into the river and thought there was something up." You are now not with the crowd but against it. You have been guilty of conduct likely to lead to a breach of the peace, and menacing murmurs rise all about you—for there is nothing more menacing than a sensation-seeker baulked of sensation. The most you can hope for is that some kindly messenger boy will say " Ah, he must be bats " and give you a fool's pardon before he jumps into the saddle.

I have had this experience before, and so I didn't stay long on the bridge. But I stayed long enough to see the unhurried swans moving up the river like queens, and the foraging seagulls making routine sweeps to and

from the swaying masts and scanning the cold current
with beady eyes. This was a good enough return, but
there was better to come; for even as I turned to go,
a stumpy, low-lying boat of the porter fleet came out
from under Butt Bridge with a cargo of empty barrels
and a crew of stolid, satisfied-looking, blue-gansied men
with tug-o'-war chests.

The little boat smoked its red pipe in the wind, and
it chugged up the river as boastfully as if it had come
all the way from Port Said. I watched it until it slid
under the arch beneath me with a roar and puffing of
smoke. And then I remembered a time when I was
supple enough to beat the best of the porter fleet to the
other side of the bridge and be there in time for the
sudden spurt of smoke that marked its re-appearance.
But the change is not only a question of suppleness, I
am afraid, not just a matter of muscles and ligaments.
It is something much more serious. My trouble is a
deeper and more radical stiffening, a hardening of the
arteries of the spirit, a touch of that burdensome and
cumulative foolishness that goes by the name of
respectability and being your age. No one is free
nowadays but schoolboys and tramps. The rest of us
must conform. We are the serfs of the white collar,
and any joy that is in us must be banked down.

Looking at the river is a fashion that one soon grows
out of in cities—and not just from fear of attracting
vultures, but because any policeman who sees you will
immediately begin to draft his report mentally. You
can almost hear him saying " acting suspiciously " and
" decided to keep him under observation "; and you

can certainly see him measuring with his eye the distance
to the nearest lifebelt. Loitering on the bridge, *a priori*,
is likely to be regarded as loitering with felonious intent,
and one is reminded of the apocryphal admonition " If
you want to stay here you'll have to move on."

In the country, a bridge is a vantage point and a
meeting place, but in the city it is only a headstone.
In the city, when we bridge a river we bury it and run
a street across its grave. And we cross the street as
quickly as possible, holding our heads down and
anchoring our hats. We pay no heed to the ancient
glory of running water, we have no time to stare at
swans, and porter boats, and foraging seagulls, and so
we cede for ever a pleasure that children and travelling
men can have for the taking.

MY HARD HAT

EVERY time I open my wardrobe my hard hat tumbles out forlornly and thumps to the floor like a head fresh from the guillotine. Then it rolls backwards and forwards a few times before coming to rest—like a lead-weighted mechanical toy.

It is part of history, this hard hat of mine. It links these hectic times with the leisurely days when every gentleman wore a hard hat, not only at funerals, weddings, and on other formal occasions, but even when he was going to the butcher's for a pound of steak.

I wore a hard hat regularly at one time of my life, but not for long. It never suited my cast of countenance—which has often been called harder names. It was dressy, and I wasn't. So in due course I took to the soft hat and said good-bye to the bowler.

This, the last of my bowlers, was bought for a wedding (not my own) and worn only once. It was a country wedding, and the principals wou'd have nothing but hard hats. So I compromised. I wore a hard hat at the wedding, but I brought it down and back in a cardboard hat-box. The box has vanished long since, but the hat is still to the good. It brightened rural life for one short hour, and then became a relic of old decency. But the hat itself will never be old. It has been new for close on twenty years.

I have kept it, not from thrift or sentiment, but because I can't get rid of it. It is virtually impossible to get rid of a bowler hat—and especially of a new bowler—unless you burn it or throw it over the bridge at midnight. I thought once of dumping mine in the dustbin, but I decided that this would be sacrilege—after all, it once housed the functional part of my head and deserved a better fate. And I can't give it to a beggar, for no beggar dare take it. It might keep the rain off him, but it would put him out of business as surely as plus-fours or spats.

There is no great demand for second-hand bowlers in our city. Brewers' draymen used to wear a special type of bowler with a metal girdle reaching from one side of the brim to the other, across the dome, but brewers' draymen have moved with the times. Grave-diggers, too, used to wear bowlers—they made them look like friends of the corpse, and they could be held across the chest reverently during the service—but even amongst gravediggers the tradition has died.

So nobody wants my old hat, and it is still on the top shelf of the wardrobe. The children borrow it sometimes on All Hallows' Eve, but they always disappoint me by bringing it back. If the wardrobe were less crowded I could forget about the hat, but as things are I can never forget, for the wardrobe is chock-full, and the hat keeps tumbling out. It fights for living space with children's rubber boots, seaside buckets, Christmas decorations, and pots of homemade jam. I had the wardrobe specially made because I had no room for my clothes, and I still have no room for my clothes. I barely have room for my bowler.

Most of the other things in the wardrobe—things like woollen vests, football jerseys, and gardening trousers— can be squeezed in or squashed in, but the bowler has to be "placed" like a Rugby football after a try.

I make a little nest of soft goods and place the hat on the summit. But the slightest vibration changes its centre of gravity, and every time I open the door, out it pops. It is as frisky as a puppy that wants to be taken for an airing.

When I am looking for something in the wardrobe I sometimes put the hard hat on my head—to avoid walking on it (on the hat, of course)—and once I kept it on absent-mindedly when I went downstairs to take in the milk. The woman next door was passing at the time, and I raised my hat to her. When she had gone I peeped round the doorpost to see if she was looking back. And she was looking back. Nor could I blame her, for this was a sight that you don't see every day— a man wearing a golf jacket and a bowler. I must have looked like a Chinese laundryman.

But I have begun to wonder whether my brusqueness in dealing with my old hat is really disguised affection— the kind of thing a psychiatrist could tease out for me. For something happened the other day that should have moved me to mirth but moved me instead to anger : when I opened my wardrobe, and the irrepressible bowler came tumbling out, an avalanche of chestnuts came with it. I realized then that a new degradation had come upon my old hat—it was being used as a receptacle. Mice I could have pardoned, but not chest-nuts. The thing was deliberate.

A sudden loyalty woke in me then. Love me, love my hat. After all, I used to wear the thing. It is as sacred in its way as my Middle Grade certificate and my broken collarbone. It is part of my past.

I got the notion, too, that the decline of the bowler is only temporary, and that sooner or later it will come back into favour again—as surely as Tennyson's poetry, and for much the same reason. These recent years have seen one of the romantic interludes that are a feature of all history. We have burned the book of rules and thrown over the conventions. We have rebelled against tradition, and form is looked upon as bad form. Our magazines are full of shapeless poetry, and our streets are full of unkempt and bearded young men in duffel coats. But this flabbiness will not last for ever. The world has seen it often before, and has always thrown it off like a fever, and it is only a question of time until we rehabilitate the classic tradition and the hat that was one of its noblest creations.

This notion—in so far as it concerns my hard hat— has weakened considerably in me since that moment of loyalty and resentment, and it may have been no more than the rationalization of a passing emotion. But one thing is certain—I think a little more of my bowler than I used to, and I am still smarting under the insult that was visited upon it by flaming youth. For the insult was directed not only at the hat but also at the venerable head that used to fill it. I am a quiet man, but I can be tried too far, and there will be skin and hair flying if I ever find another brood of common conkers in the hat that once housed this noble nut.

THE PRICE OF EGGS

THE hen, like the Parliament, does not sit the whole year round, and now that the Christmas recess is over, the price of eggs has fallen again. Eggs are down, and the grocers are scribbling the glad news on their windows in watery whitewash. This is the way with grocers; when eggs are down they make a great to-do, and when eggs are up they try to distract our attention by announcing tremendous bargains in prunes, washing soda, and plum-and-apple jam.

Eggs are down, and just in time to save the country; for no man can do a proper day's work unless he gets an egg for his breakfast, and the reason why industrial production falls so drastically at the turn of the year is that for sheer want of nourishment few of us have the strength to work. The only men who get their morning egg as usual during these black weeks are those who are neglecting their children, living on their money, or not drinking enough to keep body and soul, together.

Not, of course, that there is much meat in an egg, for it is the smallest parcel of packaged food in the shop. The egg has its points, admittedly; it takes the bare look off the breakfast table and sharpens the appetite; but it is merely a catalytic agent, and its real purpose is to enable you to stow away enormous poultices of bread-and-butter. As a food it is neither here nor there. To get anything worth while out of eggs you would need

to put down a whole pot of them and eat them the way
an engaged girl eats chocolates.

And in happier times this is the way eggs *were* eaten.
From the days of Cahal Mór of the Wine-Red Hand
to the discovery of the cost-of-living index no grown
Irishman was ever offered a single egg in the morning.
Small men got three eggs, medium men got four, and
a really big man would be well past the half-dozen
before he wiped his mouth, stood up from the table,
and took his cap from the window ledge. If a man
ate only one egg his wife sent for the doctor; and if
he couldn't finish it she sent for the priest.

With eggs the price they are it is just as well that
all the railways, canals, and public monuments are built,
for one-egg men could never tackle projects like these;
it takes a one-egg man all his time to write an invoice
or a betting docket. To build a railway you need stones,
and wood, and steel, but you need more eggs than
anything else. A moderate estimate would be ten
thousand dozen eggs to every mile of level track, and
extra for gradients. The men who laid the roaring
U.P. trail lived on meat, whiskey, and eggs, and left
a chain of shells, bones, and bottles across a whole
continent.

The modern man gets an egg to his breakfast—when
he is lucky—but it is merely incidental, and because his
little must go a long way he takes it in miserly spoonfuls.
The men of old had a different way with eggs. They
tackled their eggs as if they were arriving on a conveyor
belt; each egg, as it came, was decapitated, scooped out,
and pushed aside to make room for the next. During

short lulls, trifles like slices of oaten bread were swal-
lowed whole.

No grown man, of course, ate the tops of his eggs.
The tops were given to the children, who thrived so
well on them that most of them were able to do a day's
ploughing when they were still in petticoats.

Food like this generated energy that could not be
worked off in faction fights, tribal wars, and the reclama-
tion of heathery slopes, and the inevitable result was
that men who were full of eggs were forced to emigrate.
This explains the wanderings of the Celts, the Norsemen, and the Goths.

Seventeenth-century history, too, is linked with the
hen, and the success of European adventurers in Africa
and in the Americas, which is so often put down to
superior weapons (and sometimes, by very stupid people,
to superior intelligence) was largely due to the fact that
the invaders had been reared on concentrates. Primitive
peoples who lived on such foods as pemmican, mealies,
rice, bananas, and crocodile steaks were no match for
men who were chock-full of eggs; and oppressed peoples
speak quite literally when they talk of " throwing off
the foreign yolk ".

It is unfortunate that the peak point in the price of
eggs should come bang in the middle of the post-
Christmas financial doldrums. Our hens, it seems, fail
us when we need them most. Admittedly their treason
does not last very long, and the situation eases a little
when the evenings begin to stretch and the income tax
people get fussy, but the downward trend never quite
restores the *status quo ante*, and our eggs are costing
us more and more as the years go by.

This tendency, I feel, is largely responsible for the decline of western Europe in our time. When eggs were cheap we led the world; now, when they are dear, we are losing territory, face, and athletic contests, and being outdistanced by races which still cling to the egg while we try to sustain our failing strength with such miserable imported substitutes as orange juice, cod liver oil, and packaged breakfast cereals. It is both significant and sinister, I think, that the Russians and the Chinese, our principal rivals, are still solidly egg-minded—for the Russians live on caviare, which means eggs by the million, whilst the Chinese, when they have eaten all the birds' eggs for miles about, proceed to make soup from the nests.

THE RUNNING TIDE

I LIKE to go down the quays when pulley-blocks are rattling and donkey-engines snorting, when giant cranes are lifting immense boilers, and smaller cranes are taking up barrels of good black porter and dumping them effortlessly into the holds. I like to thread my way among mounds of chimney pots, and glazed tiles, and zinc buckets, and to follow the cobble-stones through lanes of naked Norwegian timber. When you are tired of symbols there is healing in things.

I like the noises of the quayside : the lawnmower rattle of the little trucks, the wheezing of the steam wagons, the slither and fall of mountains of coal, the skirl of the dipping seagulls, the lap of the tide. It all means life. Invoices and manifests and bills of lading are nothing but black marks on white paper, and bank balances have meaning only for those who know the codes. But the bustle and chaos of the quayside is the real thing. It is the stuff of life.

When we were children we always knew the shadow from the substance. We loved the cargoes and the clangour, and we hated " sums ". And then we grew up into a grim world in which there was nothing but " sums ". We called them trial balances, and demand notes, and profit-and-loss accounts, but the labels were a thin disguise—they were still sums. We changed everything into one thing, and that one thing was nothing

60

at all, for if we burned all the ledgers here and now we would destroy nothing but paper and binding. There is no distinction between sandalwood and cedarwood when you cost them in cubic feet, and sweet white wine has no bouquet in a monthly statement. There is no such thing as " real arithmetic ", no matter what the schoolmasters say : a figure is always a figure, and men become bankrupt not in goods but in noughts and crosses.

This is why it is good, once in a while, to go down to the cellar, or the warehouse, or—best of all—to the quays, and ease the stranglehold of these accursed " sums "; to get away from words and figures and make contact with things. And anything that men buy and sell and that boats carry will do—Canary bananas and fuel oil, steel pipes and spices, galvanised bolts and superphosphate : things with a smell or a ring or a rattle, things you can see and feel and touch.

And the ships themselves have the same air of reality as their cargoes. There is no shame in them, no anonymity. When you see a strange man you have to guess, but when you see a strange ship you have the whole story, for a ship sails under its own name and under its own flag and is not ashamed of its home town. All this, I am sure, is regulated by maritime law, but I like to think that it comes from a fierce pride and loyalty, and that ships, although they are tramps by nature, are constant in their affections and never tire of proclaiming that there is no place like home.

And as it is with the ships, so also with the men who serve them : for a man belongs to a ship in a way that he can never belong to a ledger, and, as the song says, there is something about a sailor. But to see a sailor properly you must see him when he is leaning over the side of a berthed ship, leaving it to others to load or unload the cargo, and looking as detached as a farmer leaning on his own gate when the harvest is in. And when I say this I am thinking, not of braided captains, but of the ordinary seaman of the ordinary ships that follow the coastwise lights. Their business is with deep waters and they are indentured to the running tide. They serve only one master, and when the last rope is looped round its iron bollard their spell of duty is at at end. And their bearing makes this quite clear. They move about occasionally, but only to ease their muscles or to see if the galley kettle is boiling; they appear—like characters in a play—in narrow doorways or at the tops of ladders; but they always end up by leaning over the side of the ship and looking contentedly at an activity that is the business of lesser men.

I have a notion, too, that once in a while their vision carries far beyond trucks and barrels and that they see into offices and counting-houses, into all the places where men live with shadows and turn cargoes of wheat or tractors or wood pulp into dead figures : and that then they take their pipes from their mouths and spit into the tide. Because of this, I always feel a little self-conscious when I walk down the quays in the daytime, for I belong to the shadow world and will soon go back to it, and nobody takes much notice of me. I am there on sufferance, like a small boy beside a furniture van. I am the invisible man. The harbour police ease the set of their legs, the dockers go on with their pulling and trundling, the seamen continue their contemplation.

Meanwhile I read the mystic marks on chests of tea, the Spanish names on cases of oranges, and the markings on the rough edges of new wood : and, reading them, I begin to realize why I have chimneys on my house and raisins in my cupboard and carbon ribbon in my typewriter. Everything has to be done for me. I am a white ant that can do nothing for himself. For better or worse I am a shadow man.

And so, for comfort, I sometimes go down the quays at night when the tumult of the day is done and I have the darkness for a cloak. The sea mutters in its sleep, a ship slips down the river under its masthead lights and its scarf of smoke, and a little farewell flurry of waves washes against the steps. A great quietness comes over me then, for I am standing, tethered and unadventurous, on the edge of a dark lane that stretches to the end of the world; and, all over that dark lane, the little ships are throbbing along in the darkness, taking their bearings from the stars and from their own magic needles, and voyaging on confidently until they meet the charted lights that will guide them into far estuaries. Their life is made up of comings and goings, and the world is their parish, and when I think of them I feel like the little boy who, when he was asked if he would like to go to California, said that he would like to go *anywhere*.

But I feel two ways at once—I feel lost and lonely, and I also feel big and important. I am tied to one spot, and I can do nothing for myself, but I have chartered all the ships in the world and I am admiral of the seven seas. Without me and men like me, without underwear-

E

and-goloshes men, there would be no point in all this
clamorous trafficking, and the only reason for ships is
that men like me must have wheat, and silks, and spices,
and plumbing.

But when I strike a balance between pride and shame
I see that I am still insolvent, and when I light my
pipe in the shadow of the sheds I feel like a man who
has missed his ship. I turn my face towards the city
then, keeping my weather eye open against the menace
of bollards and mooring ropes. The Neon lights throw
patches of colour on the heaving waters, and when I
stand on the bridge for a last look at the world that
I have lost for ever I see the riverside lights angled
against the darkness like a flight of wild geese.

ANGEL WHISPERS

LISTENING to the artless, uninhibited conversation of children, when they are unaware that an adult eavesdropper is about, is a salutary experience. But in the nature of things it is denied to some people, who, as a result, grow old without ever realising that heaven is all about them, lead quiet and peaceful lives, and usually die at a ripe old age without ever having really lived. It is only fitting, therefore, that those of us who have the privilege of feeding, clothing, housing, and policing the younger generation should give short refresher courses in that rudimentary language which we all knew long ago but which many of you have forgotten; so that thereafter you may treat us, if not with respect, at least with pity, and show a little more forbearance when you hear the tinkle of glass and come out to find tiny footsteps among the tulips.

For myself, I always feel better after listening to children : better, and bigger, and nobler. They should make me feel coarse and earth-stained, but they don't. They make me wonder how I ever managed to grow up without picking any oakum. For I, too, began like this. I started on angel whispers. And hearing them again I realize with pride and gratitude how far I have come since those degenerate days, and how much I have

increased in tolerance, charity, and love of the brotherhood since I took my first malevolent conversational
soundings and looked about me with the cobra-stare of
youth.

Rousseau got the wrong end of the stick. He was
a clever man, but he knew nothing about children. And
human knowledge would be the richer if all the books
by all the child psychologists were burned and the bitter
truth told. Parents aren't experts, but they know the
truth about children : and the truth is that every child
believes he has a monopoly, in his own immediate
circle, of intelligence and accurate information; every
child despises his brothers, sisters, and playmates,
ridicules their achievements, knowledge, and appearance
at every opportunity, and spends his first articulate
years proclaiming his own superiority. And this is as
it should be. If we are to acquire courage for the battle
of life we must begin by deriding our competitors, and
if we are ever to learn anything we must begin by
thinking that we know everything.

And that is how children begin—as you can learn by
listening to them. The conversation of children is terse,
swift, and blistering. It lacks variety, for both the mood
and the method are constant, and it flowers into stereotyped sequences.

This is what you hear, if you listen unobserved :—

G'long, you dope!
Who's a dope?
You're a dope.
Well, if I'm a dope you're a mutt.
Who's a mutt?

You're a mutt.
Say that again!
I will if I like.
You're afraid.
I'm not afraid.
Well, say it again, I dare you!
No, I won't. I'm not going to do what you tell me.

Sometimes the debate follows the thesis and rebuttal pattern that was common in the medieval universities. One of the scholars will make an unequivocal statement on some erudite subject and be immediately challenged by another seeker after truth. The candidate, for instance, may declare that cowboys can eat fried snakes, or that sharks can swim faster than porpoises, whereupon a Platonic dialogue will develop on lines like this :—

They can't.
They can!
They can't!
They can.
A fat lot you know!
A fat lot YOU know!
I know more than you do, anyway.
No, you don't.
Yes, I do.

After ten minutes of brisk exchanges like these the disputants tire of subtlety and finish on the simple theme *You're a dope! Who's a dope?*

Endless litigation centres round the precept that no property is private unless the owner is there to watch it, and the corollary that every owner returning after ten minutes in foreign parts suspects—and usually suspects rightly—that his possessions have been tampered with during his absence.

In debates under this heading, wilful misunderstanding is always evident.

> *Were you at my comics?*
> *Who said I was at your comics?*
> *Were you at my comics?*
> *I haven't got your old comics.*
> *Were you at them?*
> *I told you I haven't got your comics.*
> *WERE YOU AT MY COMICS?*
> *Find out.*
> *All right. Just for that I'm going to tear your stamp album.*
> *You'd better watch yourself!*
> *Why, what would you do?*
> *You'll soon see.*

At this stage, one of the young gentlemen usually issues a specific invitation to the other young gentleman. He advances his face several inches—evidently to make things as easy as possible—and says " Go on—hit me ! "

> *I would, in a minute.*
> *You would, only you're afraid.*
> *Who's afraid?* (This, lest any of the onlookers should think it was Joe Louis or the King of Siam.)

> *I dare you to hit me.*
> *And I dare YOU to hit ME.*
> *I asked you first.*
> *And I asked you second.*

The whole incident peters out eventually in a slow, simultaneous retreat that is governed by ancient ritual. Matching their steps, the warriors draw back inch by grudged inch, but their eyes remain in malignant contact until the whites begin to blur. And the debate becomes even more acrimonious during the retreat, for it takes no courage to hurl insults at an enemy who is moving in the opposite direction and is glad to be gone.

I listen unobserved to conversations like these as often as I get the chance, and I derive great spiritual benefit from them. Their only danger, indeed, is that they may induce feelings of pride in me, for though I am still quarrelsome, boastful, and uncharitable, I have come a long, long way in forty years; and if you think that I am a nasty piece of work at fifty all I can say is that you should have heard me when I was nine.

THE OLD CROCKS

I SAW a parade of old motor-cars the other day, and it brought back the days of my youth. All the old familiar features were there—the house-gable radiator, the high bath-body, and the spare wheel lashed to the side like a rubber quay-bumper on a fishing boat. Old crocks indeed! Hand me that kerchief, lass, till I wipe a tear from these rheumy eyes.

Gad, how it stirred me to see a real motor-horn again. The old horn had a mouth like a blunderbuss, as much brass as a fireman's helmet, and a fist-sized rubber bulb pimpled with red patches. And it was not hidden away under the bonnet. It was bolted to the door like a Gatling-gun, and it shone like a preserving pan. It did not merely warn pedestrians. It set them scurrying like rabbits and brought heads to every half-door.

You had to be a bit of a musician to play the thing properly, and if you did not know your instrument, all you could get from it was a punctured duck-note. The modern motorist need not know a note of music. All that is demanded of him is that he should give " audible warning of his approach ", and even this he does by proxy. The motorist presses the button, certainly, but it is electricity that blows the horn. The youngest child could do it—and often does.

The three principal parts of the old motor-car were the spark, the starting handle, and the running board. The spark had to be " set ", and there were several wrong positions : one threw you on the broad of your back, and another merely sprained your wrist. There was never a dull moment.

Once in a while, the engine started at the first cranking, but usually you swung for a good ten minutes without getting a budge out of her. First you tried her with brisk upward swings, then you whirled the starting-handle like a rattler at a football match, and then you sat down on the running board to get your breath back. Often passers-by would try their hands, and when they were tired they too would sit down on the running board.

This was one use of the running board, but there were many others. The old running board was handier than a boot and almost as roomy as a trailer. It enabled you to carry such things as overmantels, young calves, parts of reaping machines, and bags of coal. If you hadn't any rope your load was limited to what your passengers could hold leaning out, but if you had plenty of rope you could take home anything from a crate of fowl to six eight-foot planks and a folding bed.

The driver usually took his seat first, though this was not absolutely necessary—he could always remove some of the floor boards and creep in from underneath. But experienced drivers generally got in right away and let helpers build the load around them.

With generous running boards—and in those days they were all generous—seating capacity did not matter very much: there was always plenty of standing room on the outside. You could carry five or six steerage passengers without any bother, and when you passed the school at three o'clock you collected boys and girls the way a radiator collects midges, and went down the road festooned with scholars.

In the old days, if you were tinkering at your engine of an evening, the folk who came to watch you do it had somewhere to sit, and the running board was as good as a club. It gathered occupants as surely as a low window-sill or a stone wall near a forge. It attracted men who were going nowhere and were ready to fold up into the nearest seat. They nodded once to the host, knocked out their pipes on the running board, and then began to pare off slivers of plug tobacco.

Some of the people who stood to watch these old cars go by the other day may have wondered why so many of them have been maintained in good running order. The obvious answer, of course, is that they are part of our folklore, and therefore worth preserving. But it may possibly be a little too obvious, for warming pans and penny-farthing bicycles, which are also part of our folklore, have become museum pieces, and blood-sucker trousers are as scarce as beaver hats. My own guess is that most of these old cars have been preserved by men who are tired of television and who do not like to have to sit on their hunkers when they are drinking stout with their friends in the garage.

APPLE BLOSSOM

IN the cold, sapless months, my solitary apple tree
is as inconspicuous as a shadow, but now it burns
with a white flame. And it is no longer solitary, for
all the gardens as far as the eye can see are one garden,
and there is nothing in it but apple blossom. The glory
is all of a piece, and my tree has linked up with its
neighbours. I have only one cankered Charles Ross to
my name, but when I look out of my bedroom window
these days I see a tumble and smother of apple blossom.
The trees are not all mine, but the blossom is. It foams
up and out, and neither high walls nor jagged chunks
of bottle-green glass can fence it in.

When I look from my window and see every apple
tree in wreath and veil I think of little girls walking in
May processions. Boys walk in May processions, too,
but it is the girls who steal the picture. Little boys
will dress up as acolytes willingly enough, but Inter
Cert men do not take kindly to wearing clerical clothes
in public. They may look like tousled cherubs, but
they don't feel at all cherubic: they feel like Just
William. And since in a matter like this, merit is
proportionate to the sacrifice involved, I wonder if little
girls earn any merit by walking in May processions, for
little girls love dressing up, and as soon as they have
fixed on their wreaths and veils they climb up on chairs
and peek at themselves in mirrors. It takes a boy some

time to grow up into a man, but every girl begins as a little woman.

But the vanity of a little girl on the evening of a May procession pales beside the bias and bigotry of her mother, for a mother watching a May procession sees one lovely little girl and a blur of ordinary little girls. The rest of us, of course, see them all as ordinary little girls. We see them as solid or spindly, plump or scraggy. We see that strange animal monstrosity, a crocodile of ugly ducklings decked out in pimples and lisle stockings.

This is why the growing-up of a little girl is such a breath-taking business. She changes as suddenly as Cinderella's rags changed. She attains perfection overnight. She is not worth a second glance to-day, and to-morrow she makes every head turn. The most wonderful thing about the lovely stranger who steps out one fine day from the house next door is that she was there all the time. The story of the Ugly Duckling is both a parable and an allegory. It is the story of every girl. In one magical moment everything comes right.

Little girls blossom only once in a life-time, but my solitary apple tree blossoms afresh every year, and now that it is growing old and lop-sided (though who am I to talk!) each burgeoning seems more miraculous than the last—it is as if the fairy's wand had by-passed Cinderella and brought beauty to one of the Ugly Sisters. During the winter it is a no-account, never-to-rise-again tree, a thing of warts, and blemishes, and twisted, rheumaticky branches. The cat yawns up at it insolently as she strops her claws on its fissured trunk. It is without grace, without beauty, almost without hope. It cannot reflect a frosty moon, like the silver birch, or lean against the sky, like a tall poplar. Oak and chestnut can shed their leaves and still keep a hold on majesty, but my poor Charles Ross, in the tail of the year, is gnarled, and naked, and ugly.

And yet I like her better during the grey months than I like the pampered apple trees in the college orchard. They are better groomed than mine—they have been root-pruned, sprayed, and grease-banded, and there is no mange of lichen on their trunks—but their grooming does not become them in the time of frosts. My tree may look dead, but she still looks decent, whilst they are like wrinkled and painted dowagers on the morning after a dance.

Everyone should have an apple tree—and one will suffice; one for comfort, and pride, and bigotry, when the time of blossoms comes; one tree to take her place in the May procession and uphold the honour of the house. And she will need no dressing. She will preen herself in her own time. She will come to life and bloom again as surely as the days lengthen and the sap rises. She will clothe her nakedness in a sud-foam of blossom and lift her head in a veil of snow.

You may make your choice among other trees, and I have nothing to say against laburnum and flowering cherry, but the apple tree is the one tree that uses pink as it should be used—sparingly, and as a foil for white. For the pink of apple blossom has a luminous quality that gives warmth to a cold flame.

And the dusk, instead of quenching apple blossom, makes it burn still more brightly. It seems to store light during the day and give it out when the shadows come. Apple blossom can still be picked out by the eye when the tulips are lost in the night and the bronze and gold of the wallflowers are one with the brown of the clay.

And so, when I look from my window on these luminous spring nights, I can see nothing but apple blossom. There are no longer party walls, nor rhubarb beds, nor garden paths, but one stretch of billowy white that is like a vast sea of moonlight. The great virtue of apple blossom is lavishness—it gives from the full heart and spends itself unceasingly. When the light has gone it glows with an intensity of its own, and it is still incandescent when the sky is full of stars.

THE BROTHER

AN Irishman speaks of " my wife " only on very formal occasions or when he is explaining why he is loitering in the vestibule of a ladies' hair-dressing saloon. At all other times he speaks of " the wife ", and uses the definite article because he is speaking of of a very definite article. He has no need, as a man might have in Reno or Los Angeles, to be more precise, and he can make his meaning clear without specifying whether he is referring to the current edition or to a back number.

This dodging of the possessive helps him to hide something of which he is heartily ashamed—affection. He is usually quite fond of his wife, and he never trades her in for a more recent model, but he regards all this as his own private business and sees no need to confess it publicly. So he speaks of " the wife " in much the same way that he speaks of " the rheumatism " or " the oul lumbago ", hinting at a cross that is not too hard to bear and is the common lot of men—and not expecting to be taken seriously.

And on occasions he extends the figure of speech to relatives whose number is not rationed by the laws of God. He may have several sisters, but each of them is " the sister ", and " the uncle " may be any one of a flotilla.

It is a usage that has its advantages. It enables a man to boast obliquely, to praise whilst seeming to deprecate, and to be definite whilst seeming to be vague. Thus he can say, without rousing any hard feelings in the men he is drinking with, " The young fellow, the rascal, has been picked for the college fifteen ", or " The daughter got first-class honours or something like that in her examination." Then he allows the details to be picked from him one by one, giving the impression all the time that he is speaking of some deep family sorrow.

But the definite article is linked with " the brother " oftener than with anyone else. " The brother " is the most discussed man in the country. He is in the know, and he has contacts in high places. He is the source of half our excitements, and the other half are fathered on him. Sometimes he is " the brother " and sometimes " the young brother "—the qualification giving a hint of wildness and erratic genius. When a man talks about " the young brother " his face lights up.

Every Irishman is his brother's keeper, and when he sets down his glass before making a dramatic announcement it is an even-money bet that he will begin with " D'you know what the brother was telling me the other evening ? " This saves him from both challenge and responsibility, and if he wants a way out he has only to say " I'm only telling you what the brother told me " and then suck his pipe with the air of one who is being hounded for another's sin. But he rarely wants a way out, for in the full rigour of the code " the brother " has the privileges of a member of the royal family and no one may doubt his integrity.

" The brother " leads the full life. He has brains to burn and the cheek of the devil. He is a master of

G

repartee and a great man to shoot duck. Things happen
to " the brother ". He breaks his leg, backs the winner,
marries money, always falls on his feet, has his appendix
out twice, and is delivered of a gall-stone as big as a
goose egg. He is down often, but never out—there is
no stopping " the brother ". A shining brother—and
you can make him as shiny as you like—helps your
morale and enables you to hold your head up. You
yourself may have never done anything spectacular, but
" the brother " is there in the background to prove that
the good drop is in you.

I used to think that " the brother " was an Irish
monopoly, but now I know better. I have heard of
him in Glasgow, and Leeds, and St. John's Wood, and
I am told that he is not unknown in Merthyr Tydvil.
A usage so widespread as this may possibly be of Celtic
origin, but it is certainly a Christian tradition, for when
a man speaks of " the brother " he is not so much
claiming ownership as renouncing it. He extends his
roof and brings everybody under it. He shares his own
with the world. He is still one of a family, but now
it is a bigger family : he belongs to that vast brotherhood, the sons of men.

It may be that we have too clear a sense of ultimate
values to claim ownership of anything so wonderful as
a human being, and realize that no man owns a wife
or a brother in the same way that he owns a pipe or a
brindled calf or a block of shares. " My brother ",
when it means a blood brother, is merely a turn of
speech, a way of speaking, and if we say " my son "
and put the emphasis on ownership we are precious

near blasphemy—for no man is really his brother's keeper, and our children are not ours even when they are in the cradle.

This ancient and Christian concept, which sees every man as separate and unique, has been challenged in our own time by a new philosophy that sees humanity as an aggregate of Comrades, all of whom are as alike as elderberries, differing only in accidentals and having no rights or value apart from the group. The old philosophy teaches that we are all different, but all related; the new that we are like grains of wheat in an immense bin—and whatever else there may be room for in a bin like this there is no room for brotherhood.

So when we speak of " the brother " we are unwittingly taking sides in the greatest philosophical cleavage of our time, and claiming membership of a family that is radically different from, say, a family of cereals or a family of molecules. And it is significant, perhaps, that the latest revolutionaries began by coining a new phrase and inventing a new relationship. They enrolled only Comrades in their struggle for universal brotherhood— remembering that the older term, in the long memory of Europe, meant trudging friars, and sacristans, and bearded men slicing turnips in monastery kitchens; and remembering too, no doubt, that the plural of " the brother " is " the brethren ", and that the concept of the brotherhood of men was firmly linked with the concept of the common Father when it first set hearts afire.

ON GOLDFISH

GOLDFISH, the dictionary says, are Chinese carp "kept for ornament". They certainly aren't kept for company. At least, I don't get any change out of the three we keep. After six months we haven't even got acquainted.

They look out at me impersonally and without interest. They are prisoned in their own little glassy world, but they don't seem to know where their kingdom ends and mine begins. Possibly they think that we all inhabit the same world, and that I am a distant cousin: an immense and monstrous carp with strange outgrowths, modified fins, and enormous eyes; faded a little and gone to flesh, and with a bifurcated tail.

If I can assess their feelings aright they neither like me nor dislike me. They give me a glassy stare, move their insignificant lips endlessly, and wave their diaphanous fins in a current of their own making.

They are never afraid or agitated—except at four
o'clock on Wednesdays, when Morsel Three's unfasti-
dious hand transfers them one by one to a jam jar whilst
their water is being changed. And even then their
panic is only temporary. They make the best of things
always, and they accept the narrower orbit of the jam
jar without complaint. And as soon as they are back
in the freshened bowl they resume their life's work
of nosing at nothing and everything, and set off oafishly
again on their endless voyaging.

As pets or companions there is no profit in goldfish,
no enlargement of mind, no widening of experience, no
meed of affection. They cannot be trained, pampered,
or talked to. They will not even give their owners that
measure of conditioned love and attention which, I seem
to remember, is the reward of those who keep white
mice. They will not come to heel like terriers, or nose
against the wire netting like rabbits; and unlike pet
snakes they cannot be worn around the neck.

There is no variety in them, no unexpectedness. They
have a certain limited choice in their movements, but
more than any other living thing they keep to the rut.
They are as circumscribed as hobbyhorses, and almost
as lifeless.

But we must grant them beauty. Seen from certain
angles through the thicker glass towards the bottom of
the bowl they are as big as young salmon, and almost
translucent. They seem to glow with a faint incandes-
cence, as if they had tiny electric bulbs for hearts. But
this is an illusion. There is no glow in goldfish. Their
hearts are as cold as their eyes.

They look their best, perhaps, when they are hovering horizontally and viewed head on, for they seem like misshapen monsters then and there is a touch of menace in their dead eyes. They are all head, like the Cheshire Cat, and as strangely foreshortened as homing aeroplanes. But when they turn away the glory leaves them.

Goldfish cost little to feed, but if this is a point in their favour why not keep worms—which fend for themselves ? The only real merit of goldfish as pets is that they stand up well to captivity and thrive under the yoke. Very different are our drab Tolka pinkeens, which become disconsolate exiles as soon as you take them from the river, and which die of broken hearts after two days in captivity. For they are strong in local patriotism, these grey minnows of ours, and they are in love with their reedy world. You may catch them in little green nets and carry them home in jam jars, but you can never make pets or ornaments of them—they are not the slave breed. They will not be bribed with breadcrumbs, or deceived by grey stones and water weeds. In spite of all you can do for them they still pine for the waters of home, and they will die on your kitchen window-sill like the gallant gentlemen they are.

I am not fond of goldfish. They are too docile, too negative, too content. They lack spirit and character. I might pardon them all this, and live quite happily in their company, but they have a still more maddening fault—they keep doing nothing all day long in the same eye-catching pattern, and they get on my nerves as surely as human beings with little nervous ticks—like heel-tapping, or pencil-rapping, or a rhythmic locking and unlocking of the fingers. They would be more bearable if they would thresh about like sharks, or tear the curtains like puppies, or sulk like children; they would be worth keeping if they tried to bite the hand that feeds them. But they show no signs of friendship, or viciousness, or black enmity. Their colour is all on the outside; they are white within.

They are not to be blamed, perhaps, for this spineless docility, for it is their inheritance. They are not only captives but congenital captives, not only slaves but the sons and grandsons of slaves. They look like bronze in the sunlight, but their symbol is the broad black arrow. For them there is no escape from the original sin, whatever it was, and they might be the descendants of some fishy Adam who has passed on the guilt of a blighting folly committed decades ago in the shallows of the Yellow River. The stigma is in their blood, and it is there for good.

There may have been some fight in the breed once, but there is no fight left in them now. Their function is purely ornamental, and their sentence is to circle endlessly. They know no incident, no adventure, no longings. They are neither the hunters nor the hunted, and their lives lack the bright spur of danger. Nothing happens to them but darkness, and feeding time, and the importunate clutch of the hand that changes them to another cell once a week or so. In their lives there is no hope and no fear, no crisis and no resolution.

Admittedly they brighten up for a little while when they get their ration of ants' eggs, but even as feeders they are meek and dispirited. There is no gluttony in them, no frenzied zest, no grossness, no caperings. They frisk a bit and nibble a bit, but the quickened tempo soon becomes normal again, and then they are as apathetic as before. All I can grant them is a certain dignity, but you will find just as much dignity in a stuffed fish on the wall of a country hotel.

If you want to feed the Chinese carp you are welcome to them, and I will not stand between you and your fun. Let me feed the calves and feel their shaggy polls bump against the edges of the bucket. Let me feed the hens and start a commotion in the farmyard. Better still, give me a bag of nuts and let me make friends with the monkeys.

SATURDAY SHOPPING

COMPARED with the epic adventure of buying a
hat, or the cold ferocity of the spring sales, a
housewife's Saturday afternoon shopping is an almost
benevolent business. She speaks of it as "my shopping",
and looks on it as a boxer looks on loosening-up exercises
with his oldest sparring partner. It does not extend
her, but it keeps her in training.

Nevertheless, as seen through the eyes of the male
escort—whose status on these expeditions is that of a
beast of burden—Saturday afternoon shopping has its
grimmer side. When a woman shopper is offered a
piece of bacon, for instance, she looks at it as if she

were searching for signs of maggots, and when the shop-keeper turns it round confidently for her inspection her eyes stray accusingly to the cuts that he *hasn't* shown her, and which, she believes, he is keeping for his married sister.

But she is the only woman in the shop who doesn't approve of the piece of bacon. All the others, who are waiting their turn (and this is a charitable way of putting it), are clearly in love with it, and are heartbroken at the thought that presently it will be snapped up from beneath their very noses. Women, it seems, have a weakness for lost causes and things gone for ever. They are always attracted by the unattainable, and even a pound of back rashers becomes utterly desirable when it is irrevocably bespoke.

Saturday shoppers are usually on very good terms with the shopkeeper. They say " Good afternoon " to him. But this is to show that there is no ill feeling, for once this preliminary courtesy is over they move to their own corner of the ring, and after that it is strictly attack and defence. The shopkeeper, apparently, is a man to be watched. He may not be suffered even to put eggs into a paper bag without supervision, for his instinct is, not to put things in, but to slip them in. Eggs are eggs, but not to a woman shopper, and she believes that the really superior eggs are the ones that the grocer leaves in the box.

Things are not so bad when she is buying potatoes, for then she can take an active part in the selecting—and usually does. Every time the grocer shovels some potatoes into the scales she inspects them hurriedly and rejects one or two—ostensibly because they are too big, or too small, or green or worm-eaten, but really as a gesture of mistrust and to let the grocer know that she has her eye on him and is not to be trifled with.

The advantage, however, is with the grocer, particularly if he has a big shovel and is quick in using it : but when it comes to tomatoes they fight on level terms. The grocer pops tomatoes into the pan, keeping his eye on the moving pointer, and the customer pops tomatoes out of the pan, and replaces them with ones of her own choosing. She discards as quickly as he loads, and this put-and-take attrition can go on for quite a long time. And even when the final choice has been weighed and decanted the customer is still holding two or three substitutes for which she was unable to find places on the team.

The shopkeeper has some chance with the customer he is serving, but he has none at all with the customer next in line, who in the meantime has been scrutinizing tomatoes with the frenzy of a beaver, and has stowed away her selection on the top of an orange box. And every now and again she plumbs up a tomato from the very bottom of the basket and makes room for it in the cache by rejecting one at least as good. Then, having insulted the grocer by inference, she hands him his own—and her—tomatoes for weighing and parcelling : and far from feeling abashed, she thinks that, having already done the heaviest part of the work for him, she should be entitled to a special discount.

When personal selection of this kind is not practicable, the woman shopper seeks to protect her interests with a series of malicious admonitions. She says " Give me good ones, now ", or " See and pick them for me ", or

" I hope they're better than last week's." Or she
rummages strenuously among a number of perfectly
good cabbages and asks " Are these all you have left ? "
Having been assured on this point, she selects the best
cabbage, picks it up, gives it a look that should wither
it on the spot, and asks its price. When she hears the
price she says " What ? " and when she hears it again
she says " Tenpence for that ! "

In the face of all this provocation the shopkeeper
remains calm and unruffled. I often wonder at his
serenity and self-control. Perhaps this is the kind of
thing they teach at grocers' summer schools.

The affair should end with one side or other sending
for the police. But it doesn't. It ends, as it begins,
with an exchange of courtesies. The shopkeeper's eggs,
tomatoes, bacon, tea, and potatoes have been condemned
as unfit for human consumption, and he has been accused
publicly of malpractice, but he bears no ill will. He
flicks a crumb off his counter good-humouredly, rubs
his hands together, and agrees that we have had no
summer to speak of.

SEATS IN THE SQUARE

THE seats that have their backs to the railings of the square got a coat of paint recently, and now they are as green as the trees within—making me think of a club that has been freshened up for the summer season. And the comparison has something of fact as well as of fancy; anyone may sit on the seats round the square, and there are casuals who come and go, but the regular sitters are elderly gentlemen who have outgrown the folly of work.

Gathering time is just after ten o'clock Mass, for these shiny pensioners put duty before pleasure and are anxious to ensure their good standing in the world to come; and though they come here every fine morning, and are always punctual, the manner of their arrival gives the whole business a fortuitous air. They come singly and seem to be going nowhere in particular; there is no eagerness, no urgency, no suggestion of a planned rendezvous. They look at the seats as if they had then and there discovered them for the first time, as if the iron stanchions had grown out of the concrete overnight. They stand for a little while, giving the impression of indecision, and then they sit down in slow instalments, remaining upright for a second or two, and getting the full savour of this wonderful invention that takes the weight off the feet and supports the back. Others slump into the seats incontinently—just as there are people who gulp their sherry—but the clubmen have a nice taste in this matter.

Once seated, they give themselves over for a little while to the glory of being alive, and cool off in little sighs. Then they throw their eyes over the neighbouring seats to see how many of the brethren are up and about. When these preliminaries are over they begin, with tired omniscience, to sift the morning's news, agreeing with one another on the stupidity of all who are in high station, and shaking their heads in doleful joy over the misdeeds of some vaguely malevolent authority to which they refer darkly as " They ". The oldest member will ask a stripling of seventy if he has noticed what " They " are up to now, and then will foretell the end of the city, the country, and the world.

They condemn the Corporation, which has provided them with seats, and the Government, which pays their pensions, and they wonder what the growing generation is coming to. But there is no real bitterness in their verdicts, and no panic in their hearts, for they only half believe their own prophecies, and disasters have no longer power to hurt them. All they need now is the bite and the sup and heat enough to keep the life in them. The stock market is in a bad way, but what of it ? It will not touch holdings that are too small for shrinkage; and the cost of living is little bother to folk who have not much longer to live.

Clinging to their tempered security, which denies them much but confirms them in the little they have, they take an objective view of civic and national affairs, and are not unduly alarmed by world trends. The house is falling, but it will last their time, and crisis is none of their business. They sit serenely on the touchline of life and look on at the wild whirligig.

Towards one o'clock the lunch-time rush starts, and for twenty minutes or so then it whirls and eddies about them. They look dispassionately at the frenzied ticket-of-leave men, who, freed for ninety minutes or so from factory and counting-house, are rushing on each other's heels in a wild scramble to save precious minutes. The pedestrians run and walk by turns, and look round anxiously for buses; the cyclists bend over their handle-bars and jockey for places at the turn. At a time like this the content of the men on the seats is deeper than ever. For they alone have arrived, they alone have achieved what the rest of the world is scrambling for. They have enough to eat, somewhere to sleep, nothing to do, and a place in the sun.

A little later, the pensioners themselves go to lunch, but theirs is a leisurely dispersal. Five minutes this way or that makes no difference to them; for they are rich in time; they have all the time in the world. Having levered themselves out of their seats they stand for a while with the fixed stare of sleep-walkers. The heresy of haste is not in them, and no man bids them come or go.

They fix no time for the next session—schedules are for slaves, not for free men. Three, half-past three, or four—what does it matter ? They will be back again, if the spirit moves them and the sun is still playing host in the square, but you need not expect them till you see them. And a man may miss a meeting without any questions being asked, for no one calls the roll, and two makes a quorum in the square.

But most of them come back again for an hour or two before the ledgers are locked up for the night and the factory whistles time the last wild rush of the day. It is good sport to see the ant-hill empty itself and watch the agitated hordes scurrying from frenzied work to frenzied play. It gives an extra relish to endless leisure. By this time, the evening papers are out and some glimmers of the day's news have reached the clubmen, but all they permit themselves is a preliminary discussion based on hearsay evidence—it would be gluttony followed by starvation if they were to gulp the paper now and leave nothing for the slow, spectacled reading of the night. To-morrow will be another day, and by then they will be fully briefed and able to discuss everything from " Lighting-Up Times " to " From our New York Correspondent ".

Now and then the news is nearer home, and they talk of someone who will never come to the square again. They huddle a little closer then, not just for comfort but from a sense of achievement, for every defection adds to the stature of the survivors. They are playing a grim game of Musical Chairs, but they feel no nearer death than they did thirty years ago. And they have their own ways of boosting morale, so that when a man of eighty-two speaks of the death of a colleague of seventy-six he will say " Ah, but he was always a delicate man ", and give it to be understood that the missing one was taken in the full flush of youth.

Old age is a pleasant time when what is left of it is eked out by quiet sessions on the seats that have their backs to the square. Here is a waiting room where a man can swap memories with others who are out of the game and on the sideline, a decompression chamber where he can adjust himself gradually before he comes up into the light, a waiting-room where he can rid himself of earthiness whilst he is waiting for his visa to come through, so that when he is passing the boundary he will be able to say truthfully that he has nothing very much to declare.

THE SMILES OF THE GREAT

I AM growing tired of the smiles of the great, but I can't get away from them. The new ambassador smiles when he comes, the famous actress smiles when she goes, and the politician smiles when he turns the first sod. They seem to be smiling for sheer joy, and at the camera, but they are really smiling on principle and at me; at me and the likes of me; at all the Little Men they will be meeting in to-morrow's paper.

And I don't like it. I don't like it at all.

I know why they smile, and I hate them for it. They feel that they must brighten my dull, obscure little life and give me the courage to go on living. But they don't brighten my obscure little life, and I made up my mind long since to go on living—it's a hobby of mine. It grows more and more costly every year, but I still find it exciting.

I am tired of all this smiling. I want to open my paper some morning and see a scowling opera star, a diplomat who doesn't like me, or a celebrity who, in the scintillating idiom of the day, couldn't care less; but I never do. If I want to be refreshed by a little honest gloom I cannot find it in my betters : a very important person with a load of worry never looks as if someone had taken his bun, but a Little Man with a sore heel always looks like a Little Man with a sore heel.

I am not comforted by the lighthouse smiles of the great, and I am not deceived. I am a simple fellow,

God knows, but there are limits to my simplicity. I might conceivably believe that a visiting film star picks me out at first sight as a fragrant and lovable personality, but I could never believe that she picks everyone out at first sight as a fragrant and lovable personality, or that she has an enduring passion for the whole human race. I might believe that she likes some of the people some of the time, but I cannot believe that she likes all the people all the time—for a love as fiery as this must surely flame out into some wild and splendid foolishness, as it did when Francis walked the roads of Umbria.

What is wrong with the smiles of the great is their catholicity. They embrace too much. A smile should come and go; it should be selective and inconstant. It should be for you, but not for me; for Friday, but not for Saturday. It should be a spontaneous, reflex action, not a beam that is turned on and off at will.

A smile should grow, like a ripple; not burst, like a paper bag. It should begin in the soul and flower in the eyes. It should be almost sacramental—the outward sign of inward grace. No one can smile to order, since both spiritual and physical muscles are involved in a smile, and you must smile within before you can smile without. You can, of course, crease your face and make a liar of it, but you can no more force a smile than you can force a sneeze; which is why almost every posed photograph is insipid. A real smile is infectious and spreads like a rash, but a counterfeit smile has no kindling in it and betrays itself by its sterility.

I have no hard feelings for the great. I obey the temporal powers, pay tribute willingly to Caesar, and

respect those in high office. I think it a fine thing that
a man should be able to play a trumpet better than his
fellows, or score goals with either foot, or juggle with
atoms. And I am guilty at times of the lovable folly
of wondering what celebrities look like—I want to see
their faces. But I never see their faces; at least, not
as I see the face of the man next door. All I see is a
mask, and it is always the same mask—the same stupid,
conventional grin that is belittling to both of us and is
as fatuous as it is facile.

To see the counterfeit smile at its worst you must
see it when the element of competition enters in, when
you have not one celebrity but a whole row of them,
and when the idea is not just to shine but to outshine :
and the thing becomes more revolting still when the
smilers are " bathing beauties ", wearing little more than
smiles and competing for a prize that is usually awarded
by bald men, who, presumably, are experts in pulchri-
tude. The beauty competition stands alone, for it is
tinged with blasphemy. In other contests the prize
goes to the student and not to the script, to the painter
and not to the painting, to the architect and not to the
blueprint; but here the prize goes not to the maker but
to the thing made.

One can get over being plain (I have made this tiny
mental adjustment myself without much bother), but it
must be very difficult indeed to get over the defeat of
being labelled publicly as less beautiful, and there is
something infinitely pathetic about these poor beauties
who try to get a few extra marks by smirking at bald
men who have measuring tapes in their eyes. And the

worst of them, if she had a titter of wit, might carry off the apple by looking sad instead of insipid and letting her face speak for itself; but then no woman with a titter of wit would enter for a competition in which all but one of God's entries must be rejected. This may seem a jaundiced view, but if I were bald enough to judge one of these competitions (I almost wrote ' bare-faced enough ') I would throw the apple instead of handing it. So perhaps it is just as well that I have managed to keep my hair on.

The bathing beauty is a seasonal affliction, but the celebrity is always with us. There is no rest from the toothpaste smiles of the great, and I for one am getting tired of the whole business. For the great have no lien on my affection or admiration. I am a free man, and I can give my love or withhold it. I will not be bought with smiles—especially with promiscuous smiles. I have my troubles like the rest of you, but I can manage, and I find no solace in smiles that are stereotyped in more senses than one. As for the great, and those in high places, they should relax : for they have quite enough to do without creasing their poor faces in the mistaken notion that by smiling all the time they are making life easier for me and the likes of me. A smile may go a long, long way, but no smile can go as far as that.

DON'T BE A GOOSE

THE news in the papers is not all depressing. There is comfort still if you know where to look for it, and it is a poor day's reading that does not produce some such bromide as " Man Drinks Gallon of Beer in Twenty Seconds ", " Eighty Weds Eighteen ", or " Boxing Champion Makes Best Waffles."

But it is the scientific announcements that make life really worth living. Here is one that I read recently :

> *The peculiar habit of young ducks of identifying themselves with the first thing they see after hatching out has resulted in many young ducks imagining themselves to be motor-boats.*

This piece of news—and it is vouched for by a learned society—has cheered me up considerably. Every time I think of it I get brighter and brighter.

And the first notions of ducks, it appears, harden into permanent delusions ; for the quotation goes on :

> *Some ducks imagine they are motor-boats all their lives.*

And this, no doubt, has been going on for centuries. There may have been ducks in the time of Brian Boru who struggled through life thinking they were battle-axes, or landladies, or Norsemen, or Tara brooches; and there may have been ducks in the days of Raleigh and Frobisher who thought that Drake was a mallard. But nobody bothered about them. Psychiatry had not been invented, and they just had to worry along as best they could. But all that has been changed. These are great days for young ducks.

And young geese, it appears, are even more unstable than young ducks, for the learned society says:

> *Goslings are very impressionable. If a day-old gosling sees a human being it may go through life thinking that it is a human, or that all humans are geese.*

This shows the cruelty of letting a day-old gosling see a human being. Fortunately, however, it is more than likely that a young gosling will see a mother goose before it sees the farmer's wife, unless, of course, it hatches out in an incubator, in which case it may go through life thinking that it is a four-hundred-watt lamp.

But we must be careful. A goose has a hard enough life of it at the best of times, but if it starts off by thinking that it is a human being the dice are loaded against it, and it may take to drink, or politics, or insurance. Common decency demands that we should keep away from goslings until they have discovered that they are geese.

Scoffers and obscurantists may refuse to believe that scientists are able to chart the mental workings of poultry, but there is no great difficulty about it, and it is just as easy to psycho-analyse a duck that thinks it is a wholesale druggist as it is to psycho-analyse a duchess who thinks that she is a ball of wool. The important thing is to gain the duck's confidence from the very beginning and let it see that you have its interests at heart. One way of doing this is to fill your pockets with Indian corn and wander by the side of the village pond uttering throaty cries. Alternatively, you can lie in the mud and make a noise like a worm. (Incidentally, it is high time that the psychologists turned their attention to the mental life of worms, for it is quite possible that many a worm thinks it is a Jersey bull or a tuft of Lesser Celandine.)

When you are dealing with neurotic fowl you must watch carefully for signs of an inimical home environment, as many a promising young duck has been set on the wrong road by unsympathetic parents. Ducks thrive best when they are surrounded by love and affection and they must never be made to feel that they are not wanted.

I myself have had considerable experience in interrogating ducks, though only in a desultory way, and although I have never correlated my results or attempted a formal thesis I can vouch for the fact that ducks are very subject to delusions and are usually hatching something or other—often young ducks. This is a promising field of investigation, but it would require more time than I can spare at the moment. Perhaps I may get round to it when I have the family reared.

I can't say very much about geese, for I don't like geese, and they don't like me. If geese think they are human beings, then from my experience of them they have little love of the brotherhood, and if they think that I am a goose it is not very sporting of them to come at me with lances lowered.

But, as I say, I know quite a lot about ducks, and I have found that many of them are psychologically maladjusted. They are inclined to be a little suspicious and reticent in the beginning, but they are always ready to discuss their troubles with men of sympathy and sensibility.

I never met a duck who thought that he was a motor-boat, but I knew a duck in Banagher once who thought that he was a cooper of stout. And there was a duck in Tirladen some years ago who suffered from the delusion that he was a retired warble-fly inspector. He responded quickly to treatment, but he had a relapse later, and he ended up by believing that he was a master-plasterer.

My most interesting case, however, was a Courtmac-cockery duck who thought that he was a psychiatrist. And he wasn't. He was only a quack.

Sometimes I feel like continuing my studies of pond life and bringing out a book on " My Years among the Ducks "; sometimes I get doubts about the whole business, and fear that I may be a Bramley Seedling with illusions of grandeur. And then sometimes I wonder why, if this is science, they didn't give a Nobel Prize to Walt Disney.

AFTER-DINNER SPEECHES

ONCE Orion begins to rise early, and the water pipes in the attic are lagged against the frost, the season of annual dinners is upon us and no man is safe; all honorary secretaries are looking for victims, and the humblest and least articulate amongst us may be called on at any time to shake the moth balls out of his dinner jacket and propose or respond to the toast of the Union, the country, the President, the Press, the Guests, or the kitchen staff, and it is well that we should be ready.

It is not necessary that you should be logical, relevant, or coherent, but it is necessary that you should make more or less continuous vocal noises. The important thing is to keep going. No one cares very much what you say, but if you don't keep saying it they will think that you have had a seizure.

A good way of launching yourself, if you are inexperienced or uninspired, is to spin out the vocatives in your opening phrases—not mumbling inaudibly like a man who knows that he is going to be stuck soon, but saying each phrase as if you had just invented it, and turning in succession to each person and group you mention with the air of one making discoveries.

Really good after-dinner speakers can make the most conventional openings sound spontaneous, and they make it appear, when they mention a man's name, that they just happened to look behind a vase of flowers and there he was. You and I may not aspire to these heights,

but we should at least be able to lean sonorously on each of our opening remarks and bestow full-vowelled verbal accolades on Mr. Chairman—My Lord Mayor—My Lord Provost—Mr. Captain—and all the rest. Make it sound as if you were appointing them to office there and then, and try to get an " Arise, Sir Knight " note into it. If you were to sit down when you reach the end of your inventory (which might not be a bad idea), the guests who are not listening attentively or who are paying for rounds of drink (say, roughly, half of those present) would think that you had made the best speech of the night. But if you are fit to go on, it is well that you should go on, and it is advisable at this stage to rivet the attention of your hearers with some such arresting and newly-minted phrase as " I deem it—a signal honour ", " It is indeed a high privilege ", or " It is now my duty—and pleasure ".

And presently you must assure them (for they will be waiting for this) that you propose to be brief (*a*) because there is a long list of speakers; (*b*) because you have little to add to what has already been said so effectively and so eloquently; or (*c*) because you do not wish to stand between them and the lighter part of the night's entertainment. Having made this quite clear you may then add coyly " Brevity is the soul of wit ", but make sure to bump it out with the help of a parenthesis like " I believe ", or " we are told ". And to round the thing off you can coin a flaming epigram and say " The chief duties of an after-dinner speaker are to stand up, speak up, and shut up." This one never misfires.

But do not be content with a bald statement : say " The chief duties of an after-dinner speaker, I need not remind you." The aside will make them howl. Indeed, in a good after-dinner speech everything must be suitably qualified. Thus you can say " If I may be permitted " (giving the impression that, in the past, lesser men have not been permitted), or " If the chairman will allow me " (though the chairman, not being a prophet, has no way of stopping you, unless he taps you on the noggin with a bottle of Barsac).

And when you touch on any contentious subject you must say that you have no wish to be contentious. Then you can dress up this basic statement with " Far be it from me " and " This, perhaps, is not a suitable occasion ".

Another hint which beginners will find useful is that the really important part of a speech should come early in play and be prefaced by " In conclusion ", for you can always get rapt attention if the audience thinks that you are on the point of sitting down, and even the chatterers at the end of the table will set down their glasses and get ready to clap. Remember, too, that " In conclusion " does not commit you to anything, for you still have " Finally ", " Before I finish ", and " I have, I fear, trespassed on your good nature " (cries of " No ").

Stories always go down well, provided that they are not dragged in baldly—there must be some attempt at linking them with what has gone before. Thus you can always say : " The remarks of the last speaker on the subject of phosphatic manures (the bank rate, deep breathing, post-primary education, or central heating) remind me of the old story about the professor who lost his goloshes." But never rush into a story—hover for a little while on the brink. Say " Many of you, no doubt, will have heard this one before."

The attendance at an annual dinner may be divided roughly into three groups : (*a*) those who know that they will be expected to say something, and get no good of the dinner; (*b*) those who enjoy the dinner, but get no good of the speeches (because they feel that they could do better themselves); and (*c*) those who are so far away from the speakers' table that they spend the time swapping stories and so enjoy themselves thoroughly. (The third group is not absolutely necessary, but it is well to have someone to clap.)

If you belong to the third group, and most of us do, you can make friends for life amongst the mammon of iniquity by going up to each speaker in turn, when you get the opportunity, and saying : " Splendid—wonderful —never heard better—best speech of the night ! " If you do this you will make everybody happy, for even the best speakers like to be told that they have done well, and the worst have no idea how bad they really are. We pass this way but once, and we should miss no opportunity of doing a kindness and bringing a ray of sunshine into this grey world. Besides, you never know when you will be looking for a nomination for one of the boys.

BIRD ALONE

THE calling-up class was unusually heavy this year, and the Compulsory Attendance Act ravaged our suburban road at one swoop, so that now, except at lunch time, and after four in the evening, ours is a deserted village. The pint-sized folk who made it noisy all the summer have turned overnight into husky educational conscripts, who call each other by their surnames, and set off each morning dragging their feet and their coats behind them.

There is nobody left now but the Little Man Next Door. He is bird alone these days, as solitary as the little boy whose lame foot prevented him from keeping up with the children who followed the Pied Piper—as solitary, and just as sorry for himself. " The music stopped, and I stood still, left alone outside the hill."

In the morning he escorts each successive group of undergraduates (for they have a strict caste system and travel in batches) to the turn of the road. Junior Infant goes with Junior Infant, and Senior Infant goes with Senior Infant; and the Little Man goes with all. His escort duties over, he watches men who are backing cars out of garages, and who have to watch him even more carefully than he watches them. Finally, he comes back to his own gate and wonders what the world is coming to.

Centuries later the postman appears with the second delivery, and the Little Man goes with him from house to house as long as he lasts. But this interlude is soon over, and there is nothing left then but the silence. It is a long, long day for the Last of the Mohicans.

Once in a while he is sent to the shop for messages—but only in emergencies, for he is not very good at messages yet. He dawdles going and he dawdles coming, and as he doesn't top the counter he is often twenty minutes in the shop before anyone notices him—unless, of course, when he upsets a basket of tomatoes.

He has a bad record for losing change, he has broken eggs in his time, and he sometimes stops on the way home to feed stray dogs with pieces clawed from a fresh loaf. Besides, he often brings the wrong message, or goes to the wrong shop for the right message, and he is usually so long in coming that search parties have to be sent for him.

He was in great luck last week when a task-force of telephone men arrived. They straddled the place with wires for a day or two, dug mighty holes, and suffered the Little Man to fill their black billycans and break bread with them under the tarpaulin. So for once he didn't give two hoots about the Compulsory Education Act. But it was too good to last. We adults think that ours is always occupied territory—if it isn't the telephones it's the gas, and the water men come as soon as the electricity men go—but the Little Man finds it a long time between invasions.

In the absence of distractions he does the best he can. He makes desperate sallies on his lopsided tricycle, and he keeps a sharp look-out for old women selling flowers or men who offer the highest prices for old clothes. But what he really wants is folk as mobile as himself, and the able-bodied are in short supply. There is nothing on offer but a spatter of bottle-suckers in prams and two or three wobbly toddlers who operate on a short tether and are denied the run of the road. The troops are all away on manœuvres; preparing for the battle of life and rolling out plasticine worms. The lads of the village are gone, and the Little Man is utterly alone.

The mornings are bad enough, but it is the afternoons that break his heart. He hates the dual day, which divides eternity into two long eternities and multiplies partings, and when he sees the troops go off for the second time in the same day he feels that he is lost in a desert where nothing stirs but himself.

It is then, in desperation, that he begins to knock manfully at doors : ostensibly to know if Mary is in or if Dick is coming out, but really so that he can shatter the silence and solace himself with human speech. Now and again his knocks earn him sympathy and hospitality, and he may get a currant bun hot from the oven, or a look at the goldfish. But usually he gets short shrift, and sometimes his knock isn't even answered—for he is given away by his shadow on the glass panel of the door, and dish-washing mothers have no time for light conversation with Little Men. But he takes rebuffs philosophically, and if he fails at one house he tries the next. He does his rounds, and is grateful for small mercies. At the very worst, he reminds the neighbourhood that he is still in circulation.

K

Washing days are the worst, for nobody wants him
on washing days. Nobody wants him—though he wants
everybody—and in his hunger for human company he
is often forced to lower his standards and hold conversation through closed garden gates with the tethered mites
within. But this is poor comfort, and these are dangerous
pastures. He may share a sticky biscuit, or get a suck
of a lollipop, but there is always the danger that the
donor will repent of his generosity presently and raise
a howl when he finds himself in reduced circumstances—
whereupon his mother will rush out thinking that he
has been robbed. And in a situation like this there is
no justice for the Little Man. His explanations will be
cut short and his guilt assumed, and he will be sent
peremptorily about his business.

And the tragedy is that he has no business, that he
is between jobs and waiting for a vacancy. He has had
playmates, he has had companions, but they are gone,
the old familiar faces. They are all gone, and they
won't be back until twenty minutes past three.

And in one sense they will never be back, for they
have changed out of all recognition. They have grown
from things to abstractions, they have tasted the heady
wine of pure number, and they know with a frightening
certainty that four from six leaves two. The Little Man
still meets them at the corner when school is out, but
there has been a change in his status as well as in theirs.
He used to be an equal, but now they give him only
the tolerance that they would give to a puppy. For
they have grown a lot in the past few months—these
husky mannikins who address one another by their

surnames in the manner of clubmen and Members of Parliament, and stretch out the road home by throwing caps into gardens.

They let the Little Man hold their schoolbags while they are settling affairs of honour, but he is no longer a second standing by his principal. He is a lackey now, a squire, a gentleman's gentleman. He looks a little pensive then, a little forlorn, as he tries to puzzle out the change that has come over his peers and wonders what has gone wrong with a world that used to be so bright.

CHANGING A WHEEL

A FRIEND of mine tells me that he can change a wheel in under five minutes, and that racing drivers can do it in ninety seconds flat. It all sounds incredible to me. My best time is twenty-five minutes prostrate. After changing a wheel I usually need a drink, a wash, and to send my suit to the cleaners. My breath comes in gasps and there is a mist before my eyes.

One reason why I am not very good at wheel-changing is that I am not mechanically-minded. And this is putting it nicely. My nearest and dearest put it more crudely and point to my undistinguished case-history in such comparatively simple matters as putting handles on brooms and opening cans of peas. Apart from lacing my boots and changing my razor blade the only mechanical operation that I can perform in reasonable time is winding the clock.

So I had great fun when I bought my first car. When I pushed certain levers, I found, it started, and when I pushed other levers it stopped. Not being mechanically-minded had ceased to be a handicap. (Come to think of it, I wonder why they sell you a car without asking any questions. After all, you can't buy strychnine without a line from the doctor.)

I improved so rapidly that after a week or so I was able to open the bonnet without help. This was a great advance. I used to open it and close it for the fun of the thing. Sometimes I looked worried when I opened it and happy when I closed it, so as to give the impression that I had found what was wrong and set it right. The family said that I was showing off.

Going on then to the honours course I found that the manufacturers, knowing nothing of my congenital deficiency, had hidden tools in all sorts of unexpected places. I didn't know what the tools were for, but I liked the feel of them, and I was for ever finding new ones wrapped up in oily cloths. After that there was some purpose in my bonnet-opening—I used to bang the wrench on the engine-block, like a teacher using a tuning fork.

The language gave me a little trouble at first, but as the manufacturers (who think of everything) had very thoughtfully included with the fittings an elementary text entitled " Owner's Manual " I soon had a working vocabulary and could talk about " timing ", " ignition ", " the mixture ", and " carburettor trouble "—especially carburettor trouble. When anyone asked me " How is she running ? " I used to say " Like a bird—had a little carburettor trouble at first, though." This gave me local standing, and I needed it.

The " Owner's Manual " was a nice, unreadable little book which dealt with such topics as " Clutch, Adjustment of " and " Points, Cleaning of ". I couldn't make head or tail of the instructions, but I liked the pictures. They were very clear pictures, and they would have been extremely useful to anyone who could have viewed the parts concerned from the same point of view as the artist. His name wasn't given, but he must have been a very resourceful and supple fellow, for most of his drawings had been done when his heels were sticking out from under the bonnet.

Eventually I decided that there was no point in having a Manual if I didn't make some use of it, and that it wouldn't be fair to let all the lovely pictures go for nothing. But I didn't lose my head or get any high notions. I knew that I could never learn to grind valves, or cut down the mixture, or adjust the timing, or take the carburettor to pieces, and I knew also that there were big horny-handed men in garages who would do all these things for money. But I thought that " Wheel, Changing of " would be well within my powers. And it wasn't. It was far harder than opening the bonnet.

After a few attempts I managed to get the spare wheel out from the boot without help, but this was as far as my natural aptitude brought me. All the rest I had to learn.

I used to look at the jack in wonder, for it wasn't much thicker than a poker, and its point of contact with the road was a square no bigger than four postage stamps.

It looked as if it might have supported a pram, but it seemed altogether inadequate for a car which weighed (" Owner's Manual ", page 6) three-quarters of a ton, which is roughly equivalent to twelve bags of best Wigan or nine Rugby forwards.

The most nerve-racking feature of the business was that all through the raising operation the jack had to be kept at an angle of ninety to the road surface, and this called for a degree of precision that I couldn't manage without a theodolite. All I could do was to take periodic checks with my eye—and my fright increased in the triplicate ratio of the height to which I had raised the car.

When I got near the top, to make matters worse, every turn of the handle rubbed my knuckles against the radiator grid and rocked the car ever so slightly. I used to wonder what would happen if the scrum collapsed. Would I get away in time, or would I be pinned to the road beneath twelve bags of best Wigan ?

The whole contraption looked as unsteady as a house of cards. I wanted to run away from it, but I still had to complete the loosening of the nuts, take off the wheel, put on the spare, and tighten the nuts again. Here the " Owner's Manual " was not very helpful. It said *remove* the wheel and *slide* the spare into position—but I had to fight with each of the wheels, and the first time I did it I realized why they give medals to members of bomb-disposal squads.

After this dicing with death, getting the car down to ground level again was child's play. I used to feel like the man who built the Forth Bridge and think less of the Boulder Dam.

But I no longer change wheels. Instead, when I get a puncture, I open the bonnet until it gapes like an alligator's mouth, scatter a few cushions and tools about the road (much as a stranded air crew scatters flares), and wait for some kindly soul to pull up and say " Are you all right ? " I am not all right. I am all wrong. But I daren't tell him so. So I say " Can't get these wheel nuts to budge "—whereupon the Good Samaritan gets out of his car and takes the twisting handle out of my nerveless fingers.

As soon as he gets the first turn on the first nut I say to him " You must have very powerful wrists ", and then, to let me see just how powerful his wrists are, he loosens all the other nuts. But I am not there to see. I am round at the boot wrestling with the rusty buckle of the strap that holds the spare. It still takes me some time to get out the spare, but as I am much nippier at the job than I used to be, I am usually back in time to see Samson loosening the last nut. He thinks his job is finished then, but it is only beginning.

But I don't batten on him completely. I don't shirk my share of the work. I always hold the spare wheel until he is ready for it, and when he has tightened the last nut I take the twisting handle myself (" just to make sure "), and, putting it over each nut in turn, wrinkle my brows, hold my breath until I am red in the face, and say " Ugh " a few times. And of course I never forget to say " Well, it didn't take us so long after all." One loses nothing by little courtesies like these.

MEN OF THE FIELDS

THE soil, like the sea, leaves its mark on a man, and you can tell a countryman in the town as easily as you can tell a sailor ashore. Whether a man follows the sea or the plough, his gait gives him away, and it is not for nothing that people speak of " a walk of life ".

A man of the fields, when he sets down one foot, does not immediately hazard its fellow. He keeps something in reserve, and does not commit himself at once. He looks to his balance and is on his guard against soft spots and knapped stones, and so he moves slowly, carefully, and with a ponderous grace. His pace is tempered to the soft hindering drag of the loam, and he develops a slight roll from the navigation of furrows and headlands, so that three countrymen walking abreast take up as much room as five city men and are constantly bumping into one another.

In the " fine shoes " that he wears on Sundays and holidays a countryman looks awkward and maladroit. He still lifts his feet against the pull of the soil, and is surprised that they come with him so easily; he expects opposition where there is no opposition, and is discomfited by the absence of resistance. He crosses fields well, and is good on grassy shortcuts, but the county council steamroller is his undoing, and as soon as he reaches the highway he lurches like a man with a load of liquor.

He is at his best in "strong shoes" and heavy going, whereas we of the city, being schooled for easy courses and used to travelling light, walk as if a fortune lay round the next corner. We walk, in short, like the nomads we are. The city is a fine place, but all its people are immigrants or the sons of immigrants—they are only a generation or two away from the title deeds of a farm. We walk briskly because the vagrant strain is in us, because we are hopeful and credulous, because we still believe that far-away hills are green. The man of the townlands is different. He belongs to a place in a way that we can never belong to a place, and he is tethered always by the pull of his roots.

If you want to see a countryman walk properly you must see him on the brown earth of a turnip field or the greasy black peat of the mountain. Or you should see him when he comes from the well between two brimming buckets, canting himself to left and right alternately to distribute his load equably, and spilling a little of it rhythmically with every step. And when you see him yoking his horse on an uneven "street" or backing the grey mare into the cart you realize that his boots and his way of carrying them are admirably suited to his environment and the quiet tempo of his life.

Better still, watch him as he walks behind the plough, adjusting his body instantly to changing stresses, and moving as surely and solidly on two legs as his horse does on four. The tug of the plough cannot unsettle him, nor the wave-tumble of the clay, nor the bite of the reins. He has the grace and certainty of an acrobat on a tight-rope. He is not just a ploughman then. He is part of a team that moves on six legs.

There is an ancient skill here that is part acquired, part inherited. You must be born to the business, and if you want to walk behind a plough you must first walk behind a long line of ploughmen. You may learn in time to use a scythe, or stack turf, or thin turnips, but you will never learn to plough unless it is in your blood. For the great art of the ploughman is, not just to manage several things at once, but to keep erect in a crumbling world, and it can't be learnt by correspondence. Many a man buys a farm when he retires from the consular service or from life insurance, but if he is more than two generations away from the plough he will never make a go of it, and his only salvation will be to write a book telling how he failed.

The walk of a countryman is suited to—and grows out of—the kind of work he does, but it is related also to his cast of mind. He walks slowly because he lives in a world where things happen slowly. He takes no quick returns, and cannot lose a fortune or make one in an afternoon. The profit of the spring sowing is the harvest, and the yield of a young orchard may be years away. Patience is bred in the fields, and the man who turns the green sod must abide the slow maturing of mysteries that cannot be hurried.

But your countryman walks best of all, perhaps, when the day is done and its walking nearly finished. You hear his great boots detonate on the flagstones outside the door, and there is a perceptible silence before his shadow darkens the lintel. Then he stands for a while to consider the manner of his entrance, so that you might think to look at him that some great thought had struck him suddenly and that he had been halted by the wonder of it.

Presently he comes to life again, and crosses the kitchen with slow, processional gait, moving as if each separate step had to be considered and plotted in advance, or as if he had been abed for a month and had not completely re-learned the trick of walking. He looks at the darkening window and at the red fire, and he seems be making up his mind between the chair in the corner and the " settle " along the wall. But he is not making up his mind : he has his own seat, and the whole house knows it. He may be thinking of that ailing calf in the lower meadow, or wondering how soon the corn will be ripe. But it is much more likely that he is thinking of nothing at all, and that what he is doing is getting his mind out of gear and settling himself for the long rest of the night. For he has been walking since breakfast time, and he must accommodate himself gradually to the glory of sitting still.

THE COUNTRY DRESSER

THE beauty of the dresser is its clean lines and simple construction; the virtue of it, that it holds things at eye-level or thereabouts; the subtlety of it (for it is not nearly as simple as it looks), that you can hide things on it where no one can find them without special briefing—between the blue bowl and the green, for instance, or behind the third jug, or inside one of the teapots.

A dresser is neither haphazard nor orderly, but a mixture of the two, and a family tradition grows up about it. It reflects the personality of those who use it, and is a clue to character, habits, and social status. It is a legacy from the thrift of our fathers. When you had bed, tables, and chairs, the house was half furnished, and when you added a dresser—and stocked it—you had the makings of a home.

When I was a boy, every country house had its dresser. Some were green, some were blue, but most of them—and the best of them—were white, for there is nothing like a dresser for bringing out the loveliness of wood in the raw. If I close my eyes now I can see one such dresser, but I fear that memory's inventory, though it runs to length, leaves out more than it supplies. There were enormous plates on it, big as Norman shields (these for glory), and any amount of ordinary, work-a-day plates. There were rows of jugs, and jugs hanging from nails, and a gallant company of maimed-soldier teapots, each standing at the angle that best hid his deformity.

And this dresser, like all true dressers, had a fantastic wealth of bowls: bowls with wavy lines of blue and pink round their middles, bowls with bands of green or red round their necks, bowls sprigged with flowers; and they were all lying on their sides and snuggled into one another. We needed plenty of bowls in those days, for we took our tea out of bowls, and we got our heads into them the way a calf gets his head into a bucket.

There were also "tin dishes" that were used for baking, washing, and a dozen things besides. Poor Paddy Big Neil, who wasn't right in the head, used to hold a tin dish over his chest when he was singing. He said that it put "a skin" on the voice. We used to laugh at him then, but I notice that dance-band saxophonists use little tin hats on their instruments nowadays. Perhaps Paddy was a pioneer in amplification.

I was speaking last year to an Irish-American home on holiday and pining for drug-stores and central heating. "Do you know", she told me, "that when I went back to the old home I found it hard to get a proper wash. Half the time the tin basin was full of hen's meat." Bad scran to her, anyway. What did she think it would be full of? Some people are very bigoted about washing. And there's many a well-washed creature in Brooklyn and Cleveland who would give a lot this blessed minute to hear the music that a hen's beak makes on the bottom of a tin dish.

The top of the dresser was always crowded, but you saw only the things that protruded over the edge—a fiddle in a case, a bicycle pump, and the barrel of a shotgun. The shotgun was never taken down in my time (I was only a holiday visitor, though a constant one—a Donegal man at one remove), and an old grand-uncle of mine said to me one day when I asked him why : " Damn the much use we have for it in these days—we get an odd shot at a rabbit, but all the land-lords are gone."

Anything that wasn't on the mantelpiece or on the deep sill of the window was on the dresser—spools and pins, spectacle cases (the old folk called them 'scabbards'), a castor-oil bottle, a crumpled paper ' poke ' with a few love lozenges in it, and the chapel pennies. And across the middle shelf was a necklace of eggs that was long or short according to the season—you could always tell by looking at it whether the hens were laying or not.

But that wasn't the half of it. There were letters for answering, and ink to answer them with; Rosary beads hanging from nails, prayer books, tin " pandies " with wire handles, scones of bread, neckties that were worn only once a week, and a crock of cream with a piece of fine butter-muslin across it. You went to the dresser for everything from a drink of clean water to a dab of holy water. It answered every need and was the uni-versal provider.

The country is still full of dressers, but new ones are getting scarce. There was a time when a dresser was part of every trousseau, but young wives nowadays are going in for presses and cabinets. The aim now is to hide everything when it is not in use, and the kitchen, that used to tell so many stories, now tells none at all. The country dresser, it seems, is on its way out.

But it is part of our folklore, for it grew out of our native notions of domestic economy. And it did not simply happen. Long years of trial and error went to the making of it. We should be proud of the dresser, for it is as decorative as it is useful, and it makes an ornament of every utensil. Glass-fronted cabinets are all very well, but they are not, like the dresser, part of the living home. For the dresser bristles with life, and is as revealing as a diary. It tells the time of day and the time of year, lets us know how the hens are laying, and gives visible proof that Tom is still sending an odd letter from Hartford, Conn.

The old idea was that a kitchen should look like a kitchen, that it should have the shine of metal and the sheen of crockery : the new is that the kitchen, between meals, should be as hygienic and empty as a hospital ward or the deck of a battleship. There is something to be said for the new idea, no doubt, but it tends to make a woman restless and frustrated—which is something the country dresser never did. For the real glory of the dresser was that it showed more than any house could possibly use, and was not only a boon but a boast : and there may be a lesson for our times in the fact that many modern young women, having banished the old-fashioned dresser, are nailing ornamental plates to their walls and scouring the salerooms for antique brassware and pewter tankards.

DAY IN BED

I LAY in bed and looked up at the ceiling—and I didn't think much of it. As ceilings go it was poor stuff. The best ceilings (like the best people) are a little cracked, and this makes for diversions. You can relate the square on the tangent to the rectangle contained by the segments of the secant. You can give names to headlands and gulfs, and cruise through the Kattegat. But this ceiling of ours hadn't even a vestige of a crack. There was never a river, never a railway junction, not even a cobweb. It was white, and smooth, and maddeningly sane. It gave me the willies.

And then, quite suddenly, I saw the face. It wasn't much of a face, admittedly—just a small irregular circle, and a few blotches for features. But the moustache put it beyond all doubt. It was, quite recognisably, a face; and it was on the ceiling.

Had it been on the wall, there would have been no mystery about it, for in this house we are quite used to eye-level murals, and we are raising a brood of interior decorators who specialize in match-stick men, elongated horses, and liners with enormous portholes. But we have always regarded the ceiling as out of bounds for everything but flies and aproned men with buckets, and this face wasn't the work of a man with a bucket. It was as distinctive as a Corot, and I recognized it as soon as I looked at it. I knew the style. I knew the bulgy, unsymmetrical cheek and the half-moon moustache.

The very same face, only partly erased with bread crumbs, was still on the parlour wall. But whilst any boy could draw a face on the parlour wall, a face on the ceiling argued the very broth of a boy.

So then and there I had a problem hanging over me. It stared me in the face. It was right over my head. I knew the criminal, but I couldn't reconstruct the crime.

I looked at the wardrobe, but the wardrobe wasn't the answer, for the wardrobe was a good six feet away from the face. And I knew that our obstinate artist could not have reached the ceiling from the top of the step-ladder. But he *had* reached the ceiling, had reached it and drawn a face on it.

The kitchen table plus the occasional table plus the boot box plus a few volumes of the encyclopaedia might have done the trick and brought him within reach of his canvas, but though this was a possible solution I rejected it at once; for it amounted to trouble, and this artist never goes to any trouble; it argued planning, and he never plans. He is given to villainy, but not to premeditated villainy. He works when the spirit moves him, and everything he does is marked by spontaneity.

In the end I gave it up, rapped on the floor with my shoe, and thus got into uneasy contact with our sickroom attendants, who never undertake a journey unless it is really necessary, and sometimes not even then, and who tried to stave me off by shouting that it was half-past five, that the paper hadn't come yet, and that the tea would be ready in twenty minutes. So I rapped on the floor again, and this time they sent me up a boy. It was the wrong boy, but I couldn't blame them very much for that, for in our house, at this time of the evening, you are lucky to get any boy. The wrong boy explained that the right boy was spending the evening in the dug-out that he and some of his fellow-delinquents had built for themselves in the grounds of the asylum. So I sent the wrong boy with a message to the right boy, urging him by all he held dear to come and comfort his father's last hours.

He came, but not at once—he stoned the first two messengers—and by the time he arrived I was feeling like a mental defective myself, and not too high-grade at that. I heard him coming up the stairs, and his unhurried gait proclaimed that he had been dragged away from most important business, and that there was no justice in the world. But his greeting made amends for everything. It was the age-old greeting of a loving son, the traditional salute to a doting parent. He said " What ? "

I patted the coverlet weakly, and he sat down, taking care to remain out of reach of my fist. When I pointed to the face on the ceiling he moved a little further away and I could see the birth of a quibble in his eye, so I assured him that there was no question of sanctions. This was just a friendly little chat. I did not want to know why or when he had drawn the face : all I wanted to know was *how* he had drawn it. When he told me that he would be free to go back to his wigwam and leave me to die in peace.

The artist looked a little puzzled then. He was wondering what all the fuss was about. If a fellow

wanted to draw a face on the ceiling, it appeared, there
was nothing to stop him. He simply had to know the
tricks of the trade.

You began by taking a pencil in your teeth—holding
it the way a pirate holds his cutlass when he is swarming
over the side—and climbing to the top of the door.
(Any boy can climb to the top of any door, but the
builders made it easy for our boys by fitting all our
doors with jutting-out panels.) Then you lay across
the top of the door on your stomach, and swung the
door inwards until it was at right angles to the wall.
After that you merely held on with one hand and drew
a face on the ceiling with the other. If you had plenty
of time, of course, and wanted to draw a really good
face, you could sit on top of the door and take two hands
to the job.

So the mystery was not so much of a mystery after all, and when it had been solved for me I began to improve almost at once. My temperature came down with a rush, my breathing eased, and I was able to take a boiled egg to my tea.

If you want to draw faces on ceilings, it seems, you must do it in time and not postpone it until you no longer have a young heart, a young stomach, a steady hand, and an eye for heights. Michael Angelo has much to his credit, but perhaps his greatest achievement was painting the ceiling of the Sistine Chapel at an age when most of us are fit only for doodling on our blotters.

CHILDREN IN UNIFORM

THE telegraph messengers of to-day are licensed to ride motor bicycles, and are older far than the cheery imps—fresh from the classroom and new to the glory of long trousers—who carried our telegrams thirty years ago. Mechanization has given the new messenger a look of maturity and poise, as chin-strap and splash gaiters have given him an adult bearing. He is no longer a child in uniform, a pint-sized courier who has just topped the school-leaving age, but a very serious young man bent on very serious business.

But though he is serious he is not staid. He wears his cap at an angle which is a nice compromise between the rigour of the regulations and the glory of youth, and he carries himself like a soldier who wants to cut a dash without injuring his chances of promotion. There is a hint of a divided mind, too, in the way he handles his machine; he gives the impression of barely-controlled exuberance, and it is clear that he has to fight hard to curb the impatience of the boy that used to be.

Outwardly he is everything that a traffic policeman could ask for. He moves at a sedate cruising speed, not knowing when he may meet a superintendent, and keeps a nice mannerly note in his exhaust. He seldom leans hard on the throttle, and he is courteous to old ladies at crossings. He sits bolt upright in the saddle, rarely slips into a racing crouch, and tilts no more than is necessary when he is taking corners.

But I am not deceived. The paragon has been well schooled and tutored, but he still has a lien on his youth. The moderation is not his, but belongs to the Post Office, and the control is not self-control but the badge of a cautious service. If this docile creature forgot himself for a moment he would lower his head and go roaring off into the sunset.

So perhaps he is not so different after all from the boy with the bicycle. The only difference is that the boy with the bicycle was really a boy. He often had a crisis in his pouch, but he always had a Sexton Blake under his jacket. Other people's worries sat lightly on him, he could whistle a tune as well as the next, and when times were good his mouth was toothache-big with sticky toffee. He was a servant of the State, but he was also a boy making the best of things; keeping the rules of the service, as he had kept the rules of school, but giving himself an occasional dispensation and not above letting official business wait when distractions came his way. He delivered his telegrams come hail or snow, but his schedule was not proof against such contingencies as chimney fires, circus processions, and drunk men; and in any emergency he was always on the fringe of the crowd.

His uniform was usually a little too big for him—the quartermasters evidently left room for growth and for wads of ephemeral literature—and the surplus of his jacket rucked up from his belt when he lifted himself from the saddle and leant hard on the pedals. The peak of his cap, too, was sometimes higher than it should have been, so that it made a half-halo for his curls; and on hot days, when he was well into the suburbs

and away from the threat of roving supervisors, he did
what men in uniform have always done—he eased the
hooks of his collar and rode magnificently at ease. But
he never forgot the honour of the regiment, and as soon
as he dismounted and kicked his pedal against the kerb,
he was on duty again. He settled his cap to the angle
of the regulations, fastened his collar, tugged at the
skirts of his coat, and struggled for a military spruceness.

And then he announced himself. He may have been
only a pint-sized courier, but he had a mighty knock.
There was no mistaking his knock. It couldn't be " the
bread ", or " the laundry ", or " the insurance ", for it
woke not only the house but the district. Heads came
out from all the windows, and every neighbour within
earshot came out to straighten her door-mat or make

sure that the child in the pram hadn't kicked the clothes off himself. And on the fated doorstep a woman wiped her hands on her apron and turned the envelope over and over before she got the courage to open it. For in those days no one sent a telegram lightly, and a mighty knock usually meant that someone was coming or that someone had gone for good.

The new telegraph messenger always seems to know where he is going and is as well briefed as a pilot, but the old often had to ask. You might come across him anywhere in the city, staring at an envelope and searching for a road, a number, or a person. And a telegraph boy in a dilemma had a claim on everybody's services. All he had to do was to look lost and say : " Eh, mister ! "

People gathered round him and formed themselves into committees. His business was everybody's business, and he seemed to know it, for he made no contribution to the debate beyond re-stating the terms of the problem from time to time and displaying the written data. And whilst his helpers were racking their brains he raised his cap and scratched his head—with the same hand and almost with the same movement—as if to make it clear that the State now rested and that it was up to the community to help itself.

On wet days he was more than usually magnificent, looking a little like Fate, a little like Casabianca, and very much like Through the Enemy Lines. When you opened the door to him you saw the little red face over an immense expanse of dripping oilskins, and by the time he had undone his several layers (this business was like a surgical operation) and got at his protected pouch he was standing in a puddle of his own making. He was always worth a couple of coppers, but on wet days he merited sixpence and a bowl of soup.

The new telegraph boy, however, always knows where he is going and never has to look for addresses. You never see him surrounded by anxious citizens or seeking his bearings from coalmen, pensioners, and women with prams. For myself, I regret the change that has put an end to pleasant little sessions like these, for they were a great fillip to the public spirit, banded the people together, and made us think of government as a function exercised in our name. They also gave us one of the greatest joys there is—that of succouring a lost child. I have the greatest respect for the competent telegraph boys of to-day and marvel at the sure way they navigate through the thick of the traffic, but I still remember that perky "Eh, mister" of thirty years ago that enrolled everyone within earshot in the public service and made temporary postmen of us all.

LOOKING FOR A PLUMBER

PLUMBING is not only a trade but a conspiracy, and looking for a plumber is like looking for a tall girl with a watch or for a man who grows roses and has a son in the bank—you don't have enough data.

You begin by asking the man next door, who says that he thinks there is a plumber in Battery Lane. But when you get to Battery Lane you find that it is bereft of plumbers. There is a carpenter, an upholsterer, a sheet-metal worker, and a rag-and-bone merchant. There is even an Italian Warehouseman. They are all very fine fellows, but you are looking for a plumber.

And there is no plumber.

The magnitude of the crisis spurs you on. You think of the people at home, who are counting on you to bring back a plumber before the ceiling comes down, so you try Clement's Entry and Limestone Avenue. You speak to little girls playing hopscotch, and to little boys who gather from nowhere saying "Who are you looking for, mister?" You knock at doors, and have trouble getting away from them. Nobody knows a plumber, but everyone is anxious to help. Unable to supply you with a plumber, they want you to take something just as good. There is always the man who says "I don't know where there's a plumber, but there's a very good painter and decorator round the corner"; and there is usually a woman who wants you to settle for a jobbing gardener.

Little crowds gather about you in the street and debate
helpfully on " Plumbers I Have Known ". One remem-
bers a plumber who joined the merchant navy—he had
a brother who went to Kenya. Another says " There
used to be a plumber in Mercer Street ", and then,
feeling that this is not specific enough, adds " He was
a small man with a dark moustache." At this the
others look round as if they expected to find the missing
plumber standing incognito on the edge of the
crowd.

They let you go reluctantly, for they hate to have
the chance of doing a kindness filched from under their
very noses, and then they call you back to know if you
have tried Richardson's Cottages. Few things move the
heart of a city so surely as the plight of a man who is
looking for a plumber.

At long last you find the house where the plumber
lives—and since it is marked only by a microscopic
brass plate, finding it amounts almost to police work—
but you still haven't found the plumber. The plumber,
it appears, is not at home. He is at the dogs, or has
gone to Bray for the evening, or is fixing a cistern for
his mother-in-law.

Plumbers take their responsibilities lightly. They
insist on leading the full life. They follow football
teams, they play darts, they take the dog for a walk.
But they never leave a *locum tenens* to look after urgent
calls in their absence. All a plumber leaves behind him
when he goes out is the news that he will be " back
any minute ". And if you ask his wife if she knows
where you will find another plumber she will look hurt

and say " There's no other plumber any nearer than Ringsend." When you find one plumber you should not fly in God's face by looking for another.

Looking for the plumber's house is bad enough, but waiting for a plumber outside his own door is worse still. You live from minute to minute, and your hopes are raised by insurance collectors, brush salesmen, and gas inspectors. Every now and then you knock at the plumber's front door, to make sure that he hasn't come in the back way, and every time you do you find that the outlook is still bright. He " can't be long now ".

The plumber's wife and family are quite calm about it all. They have seen your like before and are unmoved by watery emergencies. They wonder at your restlessness, and want you to leave your name and address. " I'll tell him the minute he comes in ", they say, " and if he can't go round to-night he'll be round first thing in the morning."

They don't seem to understand that this is a crisis, and that no one goes for a plumber until he needs a plumber. They don't know that your loved ones are mopping up and baling out, and that they will know no peace until you bring back a man with a tweed cap and a bag of tools. This callousness is peculiar to plumbers. If you ring up the police barrack the station sergeant never says " Call again when we aren't so busy," and the fireman on duty never says " You can leave your name and address if you like, but they're all in bed."

You can always go home and say that the doctor is coming, but you daren't go home and say that the plumber is coming, for the way of a plumber with an urgent call is to take his cocoa and turn on the late news, and a day more or less means nothing to him. The only way to make sure of a plumber is to bring him back with you.

When the job is finished and the swirling waters have subsided, the plumber goes through his pockets leisurely and produces a soiled business card. " That'll always find me," he says. And we always put the card away safely, either behind the clock or in at the side of the wireless cabinet.

Between leaks, of course, we have no need of plumbers. We live on happily and improvidently, forgetting that our comfort depends on the vagaries of lead and copper and giving no thought to washers and cisterns. And then, one fine day, the terror strikes again and we are taken in our sins. But when that happens there is nothing behind the clock but bills and Whist Drive tickets, and nothing at the side of the wireless but last year's licence and a card offering to buy Gentlemen's Wardrobes at Highest Prices. All hands fly to the pumps then, and the captain is sent to look for a small man with a carpet bag and a tweed cap, only to find that he has gone to visit his brother in Ballybough and is expected back any minute.

WATCHMAN'S HUT

I SOMETIMES wonder what it is that the night watchman watches. Nominally, of course, he is a custodian of civic property—yours and mine—but sewage pipes are no temptation to pilferers, and no one comes stealing topsoil when the moon is full. Some boisterous fellow on his way home from an annual dinner might conceivably think of borrowing the steamroller, but the mood would pass before he could get up steam, and in any case it is unlikely that he would have the trick of it. So I sometimes wonder what it is that the watchman watches. Can it be that he watches the slow rise of Orion or times the sweep of the Plough about the Pole?

Or is there some old tradition that justifies the watch-man's place on the payroll of the city, some ancient ordinance that imposes duties on all who dig holes in the roadway—in return for the fun it gives them—and forces them to fee guards by night so that the citizenry will not stumble into trenches? But surely a spatter of red lamps is protection enough, and, lamps being given, why should men be set to watch them?

However, I am not complaining—God forbid that I should play the indignant ratepayer in this. If I can pay for wildcat schemes I can surely pay my mite towards the wages of a man who has the night to himself and a little red fire for company. I even find myself envying him when I see him setting out to post his crimson sentries, for I know that, once this is done, there are pleasant hours ahead of him. He may not sleep—for wakefulness is the essence of his contract—but he surely has pleasant dreams; for his is the most soporific of fires—faintly aromatic, toxic to an infinitesimal degree, remotely anaesthetic. All shades of red are in it by turns, and little blue shawl-fringes of flame curl about its edges. And round the periphery of his kingdom, the little crimson lamps—like sparks from the glowing brazier—are as soothing as night-lights in a nursery.

I am all for watchmen, and I have been on their side for a long time now. The first watchman I knew had served in the Boer War (or perhaps it was the Zulu War), and his belt was studded with regimental badges. I used to have chats with him when I went round after dark to get " the sums " from a boy in the next road. (It was a fine excuse for getting out after tea. If boys always remembered " the sums ", or at least if they did not sometimes pretend to forget, their mental development would be the poorer for it.) He used to tell us how he lived for a week on strips of his saddle leather, and show us where a spear had nicked his ear. We thought him a whale of a watchman, for he had blue snakes on each arm, and a fire-belching dragon on his chest.

The watchman may have an easy job, but he follows a hard trade. He must be as tough as whipcord, a mixture of Sherpa and Bedouin, for he sits abroad on the rawest nights and takes no hurt from being frozen on one side and roasted on the other : and the dragon on his chest might be his coat-of-arms, for he must thrive on coke fumes. But physical hazards apart, his work is pleasant enough, and the vigils that it entails are not by any means devoid of incident. The footsteps ease off after midnight, but there is always something to take their place : a goods train labours in the distance, the coke fire crackles and mutters, the church steeple tells the hours. And now and again a foraging rat will come nosing after the crumbs from the workmen's lunches, and the fire will put diamonds in his eyes.

Long after solid citizens are abed there will be late taxis and occasional revellers, and it is a poor enough night when someone doesn't stop in the small hours to ask for the loan of a match. The quietest part of the vigil is the interval between the last newspaper man and the first milk carts, but in one sense it is the best time of the night and it brings its own reward, for it is then and only then that the watchman has the city to himself.

There is a rich, elemental satisfaction in being awake and on guard when everyone else is asleep. You feel that the city is in your keeping, and that you are holding the pass for humanity against the darkness.

And the watchman sees often what the rest of us see all too seldom—the first grey light of the dawn. He watches it grow and burgeon until there is no need for his crimson lamps, and then he quenches them one by one and carries them back in clusters. After that he just waits—it is his life's work, and he has some skill in it, so he makes himself a last cup of tea and sets about tidying his thoughts. It will be a little time yet before he can hand over his trenches and his drainpipes, a little while before he can stow away his black billycan and call it a night.

ONE SHINING WORD

THE right word in the right place is rarely heard in these impoverished days, and we have largely lost the ancient gift of reaching for a word as surely as a mechanic reaches for a spanner. But if we seldom use the right word, we at least recognize it when we hear it. For it is unmistakable; it rings a bell in the mind, and, like good poetry, it shocks us into awareness, making us realize what a wonderful thing language is and how tarnished we have let it become in these degenerate times.

The richest sources of the right word are perhaps young children and travelling men; young children, because all their words come straight from the mint and have a hallmark on them; travelling men, because most of them are poets at heart.

The right word in the right place is not so much a way of speaking as a way of thinking. If you think the way a child thinks, without fear or inhibitions, words will come unbidden to match your thoughts; and if you speak the way a travelling man speaks, from urgency and the glow within, you may trust to the inspiration of the moment.

I once heard a child describe a pipe, spontaneously and without effort, in a way that set it off from all the other pipes in a crowded rack. He called it " the one like a prune ", and that was that; there was nothing more to say. And I know of another child who, getting

sick for the first time in her life, cried out " Oh, Mammy
—I'm spilling myself." This is language with a tang to
it, language that spotlights things and thoughts until
their sharp edges stand out clearly.

But a travelling man at his best—and a travelling man
is usually at his best—is hard to beat, for he is a poet
with the heart of a child. He gathers words everywhere he goes, he knows the weight and the feel of
them, and he can put his hand on the right one when
he wants it.

I heard a story the other day of a travelling man
who called at a house and asked for a pair of trousers—
which is a common request of travelling men, who seem
always to be short of trousers. But this wasn't an ordinary house; it was a parish priest's house; and your
travelling man didn't ask the priest for an old pair of
trousers. In one sense he didn't ask him for anything.
For what he said was : " I was wondering, Father,
whether you would have such a thing about the house
as a pair of middle-aged trousers."

The splendour of it takes the breath away. We whose
business is words never attain to such felicity—except
by pacing the floor and sweating blood. I couldn't
equal it if I sat at the typewriter for twenty years.

Not in these trousers.

The travelling man, it will be noticed, made no mention of an *old* pair of trousers; he did not wish to insult
his patron on his own doorstep. Such an approach
might have served at a curate's house, but it would have
been entirely out of place at a parish priest's house.
Nor did he try—as an ordinary beggar might have

tried—to soften the blow and secure a good thing by asking for something not so good. He asked for what he wanted, and he wanted what he asked for—a middle-aged pair of trousers.

To ask for " an old pair of trousers " or " a pair of trousers that you wouldn't be after wanting " (which is a sort of inverted and intensified pluperfect) is to ask for nothing and to offer nothing in return, but to ask for a middle-aged pair of trousers is to suggest a sacrifice —a tiny sacrifice, possibly, but still a sacrifice: one which a gentleman might make without beggaring himself, and another gentleman accept without any great loss of prestige. Our travelling man had not come as a scavenger. He wanted an article of some slight value, and in return he offered an opportunity for spiritual merit; for a middle-aged pair of trousers, after all, is still in the prime of life, and these (hypothetical) trousers were only one day older (since a trousers does not age in the wardrobe) than when the parish priest had last worn them; he might still use them, for instance, for projects of little or no importance—like earthing up his celery or burying a curate.

The whole affair, therefore, was not only on a high plane but on a spiritual plane. Our travelling man was not seeking an alms but offering a charity in return for a charity. No one can expect much in the way of merit for parting with an old pair of trousers, but a middle-aged pair of trousers, given with the right intention, will have its reward; and the parish priest, it may be presumed, knew his theology.

I don't know whether or not the travelling man got his pair of trousers, but for the good name of the clergy

I hope he did, as ever since the dissolution of the monasteries one of the minor duties of the cloth has been to keep trousers on travelling men.

And I am not sure that this travelling man really needed a pair of trousers; possibly he didn't; possibly all he wanted was something to exchange for a drink in the next town. But it doesn't matter very much one way or another, for a poet may take his fee in kind, and a man who could use words as this man could was surely entitled to wet his thrapple.

THE UNDER-DOG

IN our black moods and cynical moments we often
say that no one wants a man when he is down, and
so libel that ancient and honourable family to which
we all belong: for the truth is that no one really wants
a man until he *is* down, and popular sympathy rallies
instinctively to the man who has little chance of getting
up. It is when you are not only down but out that
the whole world wants you to rise.

We are all knight-errants at heart. We support lost
causes and love to see the worm turn. Let two boys
wrestle on the roadside, and the first old woman who
passes will adopt one immediately—for no better reason
than that he seems to be losing, and attack the other
with her umbrella—for no better reason than that he
seems to be winning. When the odds are manifestly
uneven, there are no neutrals amongst the bystanders.
We are all for David against Goliath, for Dobbin against
Cuff, for Don Quixote against the world. Our sympathy
is always with the little 'un.

No matter how civic-minded a man may be, he hates
to see a big policeman arresting a small burglar; and
when he sees two policemen arresting an immense
burglar he cannot help feeling that a great public evil is
being done. For public support, it is not necessary that
your cause should be just: all that is necessary is that
the dice should be loaded against you.

Everyone likes to see a good football team winning, but what really delights us is to see a bad team getting the better of it, even temporarily. The slightest turn of the tide makes us all partisans, and one undeserved score puts everyone in good humour. We may put our money on the favourite, but our hopes are with the outsider.

This strange contradiction is equally evident at boxing matches. We admire the clever boxer who picks his punches coolly and with skill, but the battered wreck facing him has but to land one lucky blow to become the new white hope. It is a fine thing to see a champion, but it is finer still to see him on the broad of his back.

I remember once seeing a remarkable foot-race in which three experienced milers competed against a little man who had nothing but heart. The little fellow started off with a tremendous but foolish burst of speed, whilst the others loped along with easy strides far behind him. We cheered the little fellow ironically at first, but by the time he had reached the half-way mark we had begun to like him. His face was like strawberry jam, and his breath came in tortured gasps. There was nothing for him but to lie down while he was still alive, but he wouldn't lie down. He kept pegging along, pegging along; and far behind him came the easily-moving milers, biding their time relentlessly.

Just as the little fellow's legs began to wobble badly, the others put on the pressure and began to overhaul him. We saw the strategy of it, of course, the superb timing. But we didn't admire it. We resented it. It was like taking pennies from a blind man.

Our hearts were with the little fellow. We knew he must lose, and we hated to see him lose. When he tottered into the last furlong he was still fifty yards in front, but the lead had cost him dear: the poor legs were scarcely moving. And then, suddenly, a wild hope woke in us, and we clutched one another for comfort.

Just as suddenly, hope strengthened, and we saw that the classic runners had left their effort a little late—deceived, no doubt, by the impossible pace set by the man in front. All he had to do now was to keep going: and he did. Twenty yards more, and they would have passed him, but as things were they had cut it too fine. The long flashing legs worked like pistons, but the little stumbling legs reached the tape two yards in front of them, and for once the race was not to the swift.

It wasn't a four-minute mile by any means. Nurmi would have done better. But Nurmi wouldn't have got—or deserved—the reception we gave to the little man who won when there was no chance of winning, and confounded the prophets. We crowded round him and hugged him. He couldn't stand, so we held him up; he couldn't walk, so we carried him in.

This is the way God made us, and there is no changing us. Our sympathies are always with the under-dog. We grow up on fairy tales, and we never grow out of the need of them. Our faith is still in Tom Thumb, and Cinderella, and the Ugly Duckling; in things tiny and unregarded, or forlorn and desolate.

This has always been recognized by the best story-tellers, and exploited by some of the worst. If you begin with a handicapped hero, the battle is half won, and if the under-dog comes into his own at the end there is no doubt of the verdict. Hollywood has done many disreputable things in its time, but it has this much at least to its credit—it has cherished the tradition of the happy ending in spite of the sneers of the professors.

The learned critics, of course, despise the happy ending as something contrived and artificial that has no relation to real life. They describe it as " pandering to popular sentiment ". In good drama, apparently, the hero not only loses but must have no chance of winning. His end must be implicit in the beginning, and he must finish by putting his head in a gas oven. But the common people, bless them, will have none of this. They see nothing heroic about a hero who jumps off a bridge with his pockets filled with lead. They want a story that ends, not one that comes to an untimely end. They do not mind defeat, but they will not stand for inevitable defeat, and the only victory they really resent is the one that is as certain as the dawn.

The common people, whose instincts are usually right, believe that certainties are revolting, and that a man must have a sporting chance so long as he keeps on fighting. They reject predestination for the same reason that they reject the classic tragedy—because it goes against the doctrine of fair play and an open field. They know that the better team usually wins, but they go to football matches because they know, too, that it sometimes loses. They like the happy ending, not because it rounds off the story but because it makes the story, because it supplies that element of wonder and surprise without which there can be no lift of the heart.

The real glory of life is that the under-dog sometimes comes out on top, that Cinderella goes to the ball, and that the favourite may fall at the last fence. We are not vindictive people, but our common prayer in moments of crisis is that the little man with the strawberry face will bring home the bacon, and we are all behind the punch that floors the champion.

I CAN'T DRAW

AS a teacher who got away in time I am interested in the latest method of teaching drawing, which, apparently, is not to teach it at all—at least, not until the child is ready for it. In the beginning you simply hand him a box of paints and let him fire away. And it seems the natural way to teach drawing. A child does not learn to speak by studying phonetics; he begins by making sounds, and after a while he makes intelligible sounds; and it seems reasonable that drawing should begin with mass and colour and unrecognizable shapes, and not with inanities about lines meeting at eye level.

Judged by its results, this new method of teaching drawing is better than the old; and it is certainly better fun. There is no fun in drawing a tea cup, but there is plenty of fun in drawing a tea party—especially if you make it a mad tea party; and whilst a child is not likely to have an overpowering urge to draw watering-cans he can very easily develop an overpowering urge to draw watering-places.

And it is much easier to draw a watering-place than to draw a watering-can. The old method of teaching drawing was based on the absurd notion that small things are easy to draw—although, as every child knows, small things are exceedingly difficult to draw. When you draw something small and static, like an egg-cup, the blemishes stand out; but when you draw something big and hilarious—like two red-headed men on a green tandem—the detail is lost in the general magnificence.

Under the new dispensation in drawing, fluency is sought before accuracy, and exuberance is more important than verisimilitude. If a child wants to draw the Grand National the teacher does not lodge an objection, and a horse is not faulted for having three legs. But my teachers never let me draw the Grand National. They wouldn't even let me draw a charabanc on its way to the Grand National. They made me draw cups, jugs, and buckets—simply, I think, because they had handles. The important thing was to get the handle right, and I could never get the handle right. So I hated the whole business. I hated it because I was no good at it, and I was no good at it because I hated it.

When I went to the teachers' training college I still couldn't draw. I used to get a pass mark with an element of charity in it for my crayon work on big sheets of brown paper, but the " still life " subjects were still beyond me. The professor used to put vases on scaffoldings of hexagonal blocks, and I found them just as uninteresting as the cups and buckets of ten years earlier.

He was a kind-hearted old fellow with spats and a butterfly collar, and since I was no good on the field of battle he made me his batman—I used to give out the pencils and crayons for him. And when he read the marks after the term examination he never left me out. When he had worked his way down from the nineties to the twenties he would look out between his wrinkles and his spectacles and say " Mr. Sheridan, 2— Mr. Sheridan writes his name remarkably well."

In due course I got my teaching certificate (drawing wasn't a failing subject) and found myself in charge of a class, several square yards of blackboard, and any amount of white chalk. Fortunately I wasn't expected to teach drawing, but I was expected to illustrate my language lessons, and I did this by drawing funny men (any man I drew was bound to be funny) with enormous legs that came right off the blackboard and on to the floor, or with heads no bigger than raisins. The children enjoyed these pleasantries, but they were not deceived : they knew that I couldn't draw. And once, when I attempted something ambitious (it may have been a galloping horse), one of them raised his hand and said, in the manner of one nominating a coadjutor, " Sir— Paddy Mulligan can draw."

Paddy Mulligan might have helped me, but I couldn't help him. But though I couldn't help, I did nothing to hinder; and I can't say as much for my own teachers, for they gave me no chance at all.

They let me do everything but draw. They wouldn't even let me draw an ellipse. In those days, if you were caught drawing an ellipse freehand (which is the only way to draw an ellipse) you got slapped. You had to *build* your ellipse, and you had to erect the scaffolding before you began.

You started with a straight line (and a straight line always put me to the pin of my collar) called the " major axis ", and this was skewered at its half-way point by another and shorter straight line called the " minor axis ". You put a bracket at each end of the major axis, and a T at each end of the minor axis, and then you tried to join them with a smooth unbroken line.

This gave you an ellipse. But it never gave me an ellipse. It gave me something like a buckled safety-pin.

Once when I told a friend of mine, a professional artist, that I could never draw an ellipse by the scaffolding method, I got a little consolation. " Neither could I ", he said. " When I was at school I used to draw my ellipses in one quick movement and put in the guide lines afterwards."

It was then that I realized for the first time the extent of the wrong that was done to me by my teachers; it was then that I realized that if I am not able to draw it was because they never let me try.

And I sometimes wonder if I am too late to make a start even now. I still couldn't draw a man on a galloping horse, but I think that I could make a shot at Errigal or Ben Nevis—if the shape went wrong I could put a dollop of snow on the top and call it Mont Blanc, or blacken it with smoke and label it " Vesuvius in Angry Mood ". Be that as it may, I feel that I might have made a better fist of drawing if my teachers had simply given me a box of paints and let me fire away; for I notice that the men who sit beside blackboards inscribed " All My Own Work " never draw cups-and-saucers, or jugs, or vases set on hexagonal blocks, and I am still convinced that a grievous wrong was done me when I was started on egg-cups, buckets, and fore-shortened teapots, instead of on such elementary compositions as " The Landing of the Normans ", " Pittsburg at Night ", " Fair Day in Listowel ", or " The Sinking of the Titanic ".

THE DRUM-MAJOR

NO one is so full of the insolence of office as the man who walks in front of the band at a football match. He holds his head higher than any man has a right to hold his head, and we hate him for it. He rotates his sword arm every time his sceptre touches the ground, as if to convey, not only that he can turn the music on and off at will, but also that this stop-cock winding is what keeps the music going. And we don't believe him. We refuse to take him seriously. We feel that his function is purely decorative, and that in re-garding himself as an essential part of the band he is suffering from delusions of grandeur.

And yet, his act is very convincing. His anxiety when he is about to herald a change of direction is so intense and so obvious that we almost accept the illusion, and

we have to fight hard against the absurd notion that
without his capering tutelage the band would march
blindly on till it crumpled against the palings at the
far end of the pitch.

If you took his antics at their face value—though
nobody does—you would think that the musicians who
follow him with such pathetic confidence were all short-
sighted half-wits; for he signals every turn long in
advance with an insulting and contemptuous clarity, and
he looks round to see that his signals are understood by
the morons behind him. He stamps like a circus horse,
raises his sceptre with fierce concentration, aligns his
idle arm with it, and tries to look left, right, and back-
ward all at once; whereupon half the tootlers slacken
pace, and the other half accelerate in sympathy, so that
a human organization works with the mechanical precision of a motor-car differential, and at each stage of
the perilous manoeuvre the front rank remains perpendi-
cular to the line of march. The simple fact is that the
band changes direction : the illusion is that it turns on
the swivel of the drum-major's arm.

When the movement is completed, and disaster
narrowly averted, the drum-major swings off again with
a majestic flourish, and the pace is once more *a tempo*.
The great man looks smug, and he acknowledges our
cheers. But the cheers are not for him. The cheers
are for the band proper, which has just accomplished
a controlled turn without looking at its feet. The band
daren't look at its feet. It has enough to do to watch
its instruments, its music, and the animated ramrod in
front. And it has to do all this, moreover, without
seeming to look anywhere in particular, for if you are

N

close to a line of bandsmen turning behind a drum-major you might think that their unseeing eyes were on the point of sliding along the barrels of their clarinets and off into space.

The most striking characteristic of the drum-major is, not his pomp, his rigidity, or his showmanship, but his courage; for in appearing in public at all he runs an awful and calculated risk. The first cornet may stumble once or twice without loss of face, the trombone may miss an entry and still survive, the cymbals player may skin his knuckles or sandwich a little finger without anyone being any the wiser; but the drum-major has no margin of error, and all is lost if he makes one mistake. For him, only perfection suffices.

For every man's hand is against him, and no one wishes him well. By trade, if not by nature—for I am assured by those who know him that he is the most unassuming of men and is very kind to his children—he must be bumptious and sure of himself; and because we all grudge authority in others we hate him for the very virtues that are part of his office. We cheer him when he tosses his sceptre with simulated nonchalance, but our secret hope is that he will miss the catch.

At international football matches, I have noticed, the drum-major is often accompanied by a self-appointed assistant who is decked with ribbons and badges and usually wears a coloured hat and a pyjama jacket. The impostor is completely ignored by the great man he is caricaturing, but the crowd take him to their heart.

As a supernumerary drum-major, however, he has certain limitations. He is light-headed as well as lighthearted, he waves to the audience as well as to the band, and his turning signals are so generously extravagant that his compass work is a little sketchy.

And sooner or later the inevitable happens : he makes a mistake in navigation at a critical moment, and having signalled a turn with an exuberance that would not be out of place in a Zulu war dance he marches for five yards before the cheers of the crowd awaken him to the fact that the band has gone off in the opposite direction. This little mishap, far from discrediting him, increases his popularity to a point that might turn a lesser man's head, but in acknowledging the cheers to which he is so richly entitled he now makes an even worse turn and is shepherded off the pitch by two self-conscious policemen, whose lot, until they get back to the railings, is anything but happy.

Meanwhile the drum-major has halted his men and is getting ready for that final, decisive sweep of his baton which seems to stop not only this particular tune but every tune, to wipe every tootle of music from all the skies of all the world with one imperious gesture. And now we hate him worse than ever and wish him all kinds of bad luck. We pray that one of the tootlers, unsighted for the moment, will play on for a bar or two in the tremendous silence, or that the drummer will keep thumping just for the devil of it. But what we are all waiting for is the day when the drum-major himself will make a wrong turning and go marching off into the sunset completely bereft of bandsmen.

BIRDS IN THEIR LITTLE NESTS

TIME softens most hurts, and you have only to mention the schoolbooks of long ago to awaken tender sentiments in the most unlikely breasts. People like John-o'-the-Hill, whose contemporaries allege that he wore out seven Primers and left school with the status of a Senior Infant, will deplore the meagre diet of present-day scholars and boast of a regimen to which they themselves are no credit; and the Man with a Pint will halt his glass in mid-air and return it to the counter whilst he shakes his head in tribute to the dear departed and says " God be with the oul' Third Book " —in the manner of one giving a text for meditation.

By the time I was sent to school, the old tradition had weakened considerably, uplift was on the wane, and degenerate compilers of primary-school texts were finding room for such bloodthirsty and immoral stuff as *Cuff's Fight with Dobbin*. But though the tradition had weakened it was by no means dead, and the verse that was offered for our delectation was clearly intended to refine. I am glad to be able to report that it did nothing of the kind.

One of the most fragrant pieces, I remember, ran something like this :

> *Birds in their little nests agree,*
> *And 'tis a shameful sight*
> *When children of one family*
> *Fall out, and chide, and fight.*

Now there are several things wrong with this verse, and the first is the misuse of the word 'chide'—which is much too anaemic for its context here. Anyone who believes that this is what children do before they beat the daylights out of one another will have no difficulty in accepting the evidence of the docker who explained that when his mate dropped a box of horseshoes on his foot his own response had been " Careful, 'Erb, careful." But the " when " is even worse; it is a cruel libel on that ancient institution the Christian family. It gives the impression that disagreement is a regrettable and occasional incident in family life, whereas it is a constant ingredient. If disagreement is a shameful sight then the Christian family is a shameful sight, and no one has the right to say that about the Christian family.

The mark of the Christian family is that its members never agree about anything, so that it is the archetype of debating societies, duelling clubs, election speeches, and guerilla war. It is all of these things, but it is not a shameful sight.

It is high time that we nailed the hoary lie which generation after generation of hypocritical fathers has perpetuated, and which takes the form: " What kind of children are you at all ? I never saw anything like you—certainly not in the house I was reared in." If you didn't, you must have been reared in an incubator. The danger of this fiction is that if it is repeated (and it always *is* repeated) it will make normal healthy children think that they are monstrosities that have cropped up mysteriously to sully the proud record of a long and virtuous line: and life is hard enough for children without making it as hard as that.

You needn't tell them the truth, of course, and boast of the day when you knocked your brother's tooth out, but you should remember it occasionally as a link with sanity; and since you are rearing a family, the more links you have with sanity the better. The truth is that all children are belligerent by nature, and the kind of war they like best is civil war—for the reason that if properly managed it can be made almost continuous, with intervals for food and sleep.

To speak of a boy's " nearest and dearest " is a contradiction in terms. A boy may fight occasionally with the boy across the street, but if he is worth rearing at all he will be always fighting with the boy across the table. He will have many enemies, but his bitterest and most permanent enemy is the man who shares his bed; he will grudge him the light of day. No blanket is big enough to cover two boys, no division of apple tart will leave them both happy, and no boy will take the blame for blotting his exercise when there is a brother in the same room with him.

It may be deplorable, but there is nothing much we can do about it. We can only leave boys to God and their guardian angels and hope that they will make a better fist of growing up than we did. Besides, in one sense, the family fight is a form of sublimation—it gets a lot of truculence out of the system and prepares a man for citizenship. The boy who grows up in a big family comes to see the folly of constant war, and is likely to shun riot and civil commotion for the rest of his days. He does his military service very early in life, and after that all he wants is peace to grow his roses.

You may feel downcast when you see that your children have no love of the brotherhood, but this is the normal way of children. You may preach little homilies at times, and quite rightly, but you should be careful in your choice of moral lessons and uplift verses, and there is no sense in blighting your children's lives by calling their attention to the rectitude of nestlings. For you are rearing a family of human beings, not a clutch of Lesser Whitethroats or Great Spotted Wood-pipers, and besides, it is not by any means certain that little birds in their nests agree. Finally, don't expect to be any better than half-cracked when it is all over, and remember once in a while, in the midst of your exhortations, that you are only echoing the words of the decent man that reared you.

AT THE DOCTOR'S

AS soon as you enter the waiting room, the earliest
settlers look up hopefully, like convicts waiting to
be released in rotation; and the one nearest his freedom
makes a half-move to rise. But you are only a false
alarm, and they hate you for it. They grade you quickly
as a case of scabies, and probably lowly born at that.
Then they go back to their reading.

They have the best seats, the pick of the magazines,
and a look of belonging. They have roots in the place.

You cross the room on tip-toe, edge out a chair for
yourself, and take possession of it by furtive instalments.
You moisten your lips nervously, and you swallow with
the thunderous noise of a trout raising a ripple. Then,
in order to hide yourself, you reach for a magazine;
but you don't have to reach all the way, for someone

inches it in your direction and without looking up. This looks like kindness, but it isn't kindness : it is fear of infection. They don't want to have you too near.

When you turn a page it rattles like corrugated iron, whereupon the gentleman on your right looks up with an air which says that doctors' waiting rooms are not what they used to be. There is a cramp in your leg and a tickle in your throat, but you can't do anything about them. You are still on probation and you must suffer in silence. There is no sound but the beating of your heart and the ticking of the clock, and one seems as loud as the other. You sense animosity all about you, and when you look at the enormous pieces of pottery on the enormous sideboard you find that a Chinese gentleman with a bare stomach is sneering at you openly. And so well he might, for he has been there for years.

You steal occasional glances at your neighbours, all of whom are browsing steadily, and seemingly without breathing. Once in a while one of them comes up for air and gazes about her with the passivity of a seal, but if she catches you looking at her she sinks back into the depths, whilst you try to make it appear that you were really looking at the black horses on the mantelpiece.

You pretend to be reading a magazine, but you are not reading a magazine. All you are doing is gobbling the pictures, and you daren't turn the pages quickly enough to keep pace with your appetite. When you finish one magazine you must meditate for a little while before you acquire another one. And it is bad form to grab at a magazine. You must take it up with a show of reluctance and give the impression that this sort of reading is beneath you.

But time passes, even in a doctor's waiting room, and eventually the door opens. This is what we have all been waiting for—the stirring of the waters—and we look up eagerly. But this time, too, it is a false alarm. It is only one more for hate, one more for what amounts to solitary confinement in company. In he comes, awkwardly and with due regard for what religious call " the custody of the eyes ". He moves a chair as if it might break in his hands, and wonders what to do with his hat and gloves. He reaches for a magazine—the nearest—much as a man might reach for a lifebelt, and you slide it unobtrusively towards him. He begins to smile his thanks then, but you reject this impertinence, and the smile crumples against your lowered skull.

By this time you are feeling much more sure of yourself. You are not yet one of the old stock, but you are certainly much older than when you came in.

The next time the door opens, the oldest inhabitant rises as if she had just been called to the throne, gathers up her bag and gloves, and makes a magnificent exit until she stumbles over the doormat. Her attitude conveys that she is glad to be gone and that her only reason for coming among you was to see for herself how the lower orders look at close quarters. This vacancy leads to promotions all round, and everyone relaxes a little. Even the latest arrival gets his colour back—in no time he will be lording it over green immigrants.

After another half-hour you are well up in line of succession and you feel like one of the landed gentry.

You cough when you feel like it, stretch your legs, and reach for distant magazines. Every departure brings you nearer release, and every arrival increases your seniority.

At last your big moment comes. The door opens (it always seems to open of itself) and a disembodied voice calls out your name. You get to your feet slowly and deliberately, as becomes your rank and status, take care to avoid the doormat, and then spoil everything by having to surrender your magazine to the receptionist.

You feel so well then that it is hardly worth while bothering the doctor at all. Your holiday has done you a world of good, and the rest has toned up your system. All you want to do is to catch up on the news that you have missed during your long incarceration.

When the doctor asks how you feel, the noise of it batters on your eardrums. You wonder why he is shouting, and you wonder what is wrong with your ears. But he is not shouting, and there is nothing wrong with your ears. All that is wrong is that you have been a long time in the wilderness and have not yet accustomed yourself again to the noise of human speech.

But all this will come right soon, and there is nothing to worry about. Alexander Selkirk probably felt much the same when they took him off his island.

A BOY WITH A RABBIT

IT was unfortunate from the Morsel's point of view that he should have begun to learn the piano on the very day that he became the owner of a white rabbit, and it was unfortunate from our point of view that he should have become the owner of a white rabbit on the very day that he began to learn the piano. We didn't want the rabbit, and he didn't want to learn the piano, but as we all live in the same house we had to come to terms. We agreed to tolerate the rabbit, and he agreed to learn the piano.

The statement that the Morsel is learning the piano needs some qualification. He says himself that he is " at music ", meaning, I think, that he is up against it, for so far he has shown little enthusiasm for the keyboard. And I can't blame him very much. The piano, in the beginning, is tough going; once you have got as far as *The Bluebells of Scotland* you have the worst of it over you, but until then things are pretty grim.

The real trouble with the Morsel is that he hasn't time for his music. A man with a rabbit hasn't time for anything. It has to be groomed, exercised, petted, and fed—especially fed. Our rabbit must be the best-fed rabbit in the country. During its free time it has the run of the garden, with the result that there is nothing left of our sprouts but the stumps, and in the Morsel's free time it is fed almost continuously with dandelion leaves, carrots, and cream. When it came to us first it was about the size of a goose egg and looked like an animated snowball, but now it is more like the snowball in Primer Two. (You know the lesson—*What fun Ned and May had rolling their big snowball.*) For a white rabbit, ours is in the pink of condition.

Mentally, however, he is in a bad way. He leads the life of a wild rabbit, but he has the mental outlook of a tame rabbit. He likes freedom, and he gets plenty of it, but he is not equipped for freedom. I think that he is becoming a schizophrenic, a split personality—either that or he hasn't the brains of a rabbit. We have tried him with shock treatment, but it just doesn't work. When you say " shoosh " he won't shoosh, and when you pretend to kick him the subterfuge is lost. It is a waste of time to simulate anger, for he doesn't understand anger, and if you interpose a broom between him and your young cabbages he regards both you and the broom with puzzled benevolence. Short of actual assault—and this he has never experienced—there is no way of discouraging him.

Sometimes he wanders round the side passage and makes his way out to the public street : and now and again a neighbour will knock at the door in the gloaming with his eyes full of reproach and his arms full of white rabbit. So between one thing and another the Morsel hasn't much time for his music.

And the strain is beginning to tell on him, so that when he does his five-finger exercises his forehead creases and his tongue comes out in sympathy. And they are, quite literally, five-finger exercises : each finger is in business for itself. When one finger is on the piano the other four are sprawled grotesquely, and the muscular effort required to drag them into action is out of all proportion to the volume of sound produced. All the fingers are bad, but the little finger is worse than any of the others, and at times it seems dislocated. The Morsel has to force it into action by leaning on it with the fingers of the other hand, and this does not add to the fluency of his performance.

In order to get him to practise at all we have to resort to blandishments. We say " When Beethoven was a little boy he used to practise for hours and hours every day ", which is not a very fair argument, since the young Beethoven had not the distraction of a white rabbit. Or we say (continuing the " Boyhood of Famous Men " treatment) " When your Daddy was a boy he used to practise for forty minutes every day ", which is not true, and which if it were true would be an argument against the piano rather than for it. But we usually end up by offering him money. Every boy has his price, and the Morsel's is sixpence for ten minutes.

But one morning recently, as I lay between waking and getting up, I heard the Morsel playing the piano—which is an agonizing experience at any time, but particularly agonizing at seven in the morning, for he plays at the rate of ten notes a minute, and they drip maddeningly into the brain. Whenever I hear him playing I remember the story of the sleepless man who climbed to the upstairs flat and asked the man above when he was going to take off his other shoe. But my suffering on this occasion was overlain by a great wonder—I wondered what had induced our sordid bloodsucker to revert to amateur status; to become, in other words, a gentleman player.

But the mystery, when I inquired into it later in the day, was not such a mystery after all. The Morsel, it appeared, had risen early to feed his white rabbit. Then, finding time heavy on his hands, he spent it at the piano—getting in a little overtime at the usual rates (if he were properly organized he would demand time-and-a-half), and reminding the people upstairs that he was ready for his breakfast.

I am reluctant to discourage this early-morning practice, for though it is desultory it is still practice, but I am afraid that I may have to do something about it—even at the risk of stifling a budding Mozart. I could overlook the breadcrumbs that we find between the keys, and the red stains (which might well be the Morsel's heart's blood but are only " This Season's Strawberry "), but the smell is quite another thing. It is a strong smell, though not altogether unpleasant, and I was a little time identifying it. I thought at first that it was rancid furniture cream, but it isn't the smell of furniture cream—it is the kind of smell that you get from a poacher's pocket or from the inside of a conjuror's tall hat.

LITTLE NOSES

A SAYING which caught my eye in an American magazine some time ago went something like this:

> "His clothes may be shabby and his hat shiny, but if his children have their noses pressed against the window-pane when it is time for him to come home you can trust him with everything you have."

At first sight it looks fair enough, but it contains at least two blunders. In the first place, "may" is far too weak a word in its context, for a man who supports a house full of little noses is bound to be shabby and shiny. He has made his choice. He can't have everything, and until the little noses are big enough to keep themselves in hankies he is lucky to have anything.

But the second blunder is more serious, and it is the easy assumption that a child with his nose pressed against the window-pane is there because he loves his father, whereas he may be making faces at the passers-by or cooling off for a minute or two before he pulls more stuffing out of the settee. He may also be just enjoying the feel of cold glass against his nose (you should try it some time) or taking his turn on sentry-go: if children are to grow up properly they just can't have adults walking in unannounced.

A row of children's noses at the window-pane sometimes means a row of determined and habitual litigants,

each of whom is ready to double as plaintiff and defend-
ant. Every nose there, as likely as not, has information
to lay against its fellows and wants to be first in the
field. This is why fathers of families have no trouble
in following the reports of court libel actions, in which
the usual defence is that I did not call the plaintiff a
blue-nosed baboon, but if I did it was a privileged
occasion and fair comment.

I am not suggesting, of course, that a child who waits
at the window is not fond of his father, and I agree
that one of the loveliest things in the world is to have
children waiting for you when you come home from
work. But it is also a reminder that you are only in
for re-charging, and that as soon as you get some food
and rest you will have to put on your shiny hat again
and go out to earn more money.

And before you preen yourself because a row of noses
greets you at the window it is well to be sure that it is
you they are waiting for. Sometimes they are waiting
for you, but usually they are waiting for lollipops, or to
borrow your pencil. You just can't be sure whether
they are waiting or lying in wait.

Children sometimes run to the gate to meet their
father, but usually they wait until he enters the hall—
they can get at him better there. And if they make
for his hand it is only to prise the evening paper out
of it, for though a father may be a popular feature in
his home he is not nearly as popular a feature as the
strip cartoon.

Once a father has been shorn of his paper there is
nothing left of him but the husk. The only one who

o

takes any notice of him then is the one who is "next on" the paper and who maintains that the nose who has it at the moment is not making good enough time.

When the father has hung up his shiny coat, and washed his horny hands, he approaches his armchair—only to find that it is already occupied by a young pretender, and before he sits down he has to stage an eviction. The usurper vacates the throne willingly enough and makes no demur—this much must be said to his credit. Then he stretches himself full-length on the hearthrug, and goes on with his reading.

I agree that a man with shabby clothes and a spatter of little noses can be trusted. I go further and say that he cannot even be tempted. You will never find him leading insurrections, and there is no danger at all in leaving him with the petty cash. For he is tethered and spancelled; he has given hostages; he just can't get away. He has neither the leisure nor the energy to think out iniquities. He has a bigger stake in the country than anybody else, and he can't forget it because he is tied to it.

The shabby man who has enough children to justify and explain his shabbiness is society's greatest stabiliser. He is a stay on civil commotion, a conservative influence, an upholder of the *status quo*. In short, he is a solid man. Most of what he earns goes on noses, his dress suit never leaves the hanger, and he wouldn't know an orchid from a hibiscus. All his money is in livestock, and his investments won't mature until they are no longer investments.

But he has mighty consolations, and he doesn't regret his lost freedom. He lives from crisis to crisis and never knows what he will find in front of him when the day's work is done. And he is always glad to see a row of noses pressed against the window-pane when he comes home in the evening—provided that none of them is missing. For even one missing white button raises dreadful possibilities. The owner may be doing his home exercise, or have gone to the grocer's for a pound of sausages, but he may also be in hospital, or even in jail. You just never know.

THE HORSE

ONE of the first essays I ever wrote was an essay
on " The Horse "; and I would like to add some
footnotes to it now. It wasn't my essay, of course—
it was a classic long before I was born. It came down
to me through long generations of teachers and pupils,
and it began something like this : " The horse is a
noble animal. He is man's best friend. He has four
legs, and he ploughs the farmer's fields." It was a
wonderful opening, for most of it could be used again
in an essay on " The Dog ". The old schoolmasters
knew what they were about.

Most of the essay was given to us beforehand, either
by way of a preliminary talk or of blackboard " heads ",
but self-expression was encouraged, and after a para-
graph or two you were on your own. I wish I could
remember my essay, but all I can do is quote from a
recent effort by Morsel Two—which proves that genius
runs in families :

> " It eats hay and otes and the forge is a busy
> place. A young horse is called a fole. The horse
> does not grow wool like the sheep and he is no
> good when he is dead. A horse soldier is called
> cavalry and is used to fight battles but not now.
> The flesh of the sheep is called mutton. Horses
> are very strong and it is man's best friend."

But Morsel Two is almost the last of his line, and
before very long the boy who writes on " The Horse "

will be writing a requiem. Even now, the horse belongs only to the little fields, and—surprisingly enough—to the cities : the big fields have banished him long since.

One day this week I looked over a hedge into a twenty-acre field that was being got ready for the spring sowing. Two mechanical cultivators were churning the brown earth and spilling it into stiff, slow-crumbling swathes. And it was no bother to them—they did it as easily as an electric mixer makes cake-batter in a bowl.

A man could look for long enough into a field like this one nowadays and never see a horse. The old grey mare is dead and gone, and the farmer's boy is a rare hand with a spanner.

But there are still a few horses left in the city, and when I look at them I find it hard to improve on the old essay that we all wrote long ago. For the horse is still a noble animal; he may be on the way out, but he holds his head high.

The racehorse is too skinny for my liking. He has been bred by the book and worked out like a formula. He is a little bit too fine, a little bit too sensitive. For choice, give me the great-thewed draught horse, with square flanks, and solid legs, and fringes of hair round his ankles. His immense back is slightly concave, the corded veins stand out under the skin of his belly, and his neck arches like a taut bow against the tug of the reins and the pull of the load.

And in his harness he is like a knight girded for battle. For his harness is no shame to him : it sets off his strength and bulk without taking too much from his dignity. (But I am sorry about his blinkers—for they give him the look of a mildly moidered granny in a sun bonnet, and the drayman sometimes makes things worse by sticking in a rose for trimming.)

We take harness for granted, but it has centuries of tradition behind it and is most cunningly contrived. It was no simple matter in the beginning to hold a horse without hampering him, to devise a pattern of straps and hooks and pads that would spread the strain from tail to shoulder and sustain this immense bulk of flesh as surely as a line holds a hooked salmon.

As I say, I like enormous horses, and I also like the men who work with enormous horses. Jockeys are all very well, but there is not enough of them in it, and part of their conditions of employment is that they should be constantly on the verge of disappearing. Your city lorry-driver, now, is a different breed, and he may put on weight with impunity. He is sure of himself, and his confidence shows in his face. He sits on a throne of folded sacks and enjoys the priority that the traffic laws give him; for the horse came first, and it still comes first. It plods along with its head down and all lesser things must give it place.

The stance and demeanour of a lorry-driver—especially when, having delivered a package, he thumbs through his dockets to collect a signature—proclaim his independence. He obeys, but he gives only a limited obedience, and he does not concern himself unduly with the business of his employers. He accepts the position that, for reasons outside his ken, certain things have to be moved from place to place, and he is ready to earn a living by moving them; but he makes it clear that errors and omissions are no concern of his and keeps

to the letter of his contract. If you want the stuff you must sign for it, and if you don't, it is all the same to him. He will plank a bale on your doorstep, but after that he takes no responsibility for anything but his horse.

To me, one of the most amazing things about a horse is the passive way in which he stands for his shoeing. He lets the blacksmith take his whiskered hoofs one by one into his aproned lap, and he makes no complaint when the metal burns out a bed for itself and the nails are driven home. His whole nature seems changed, and his fire is replaced by trust and docility.

Taming the horse was a wonderful adventure, but putting shoes on him was more wonderful still. And there must have been a first time; there must have been, in some time and in some place, a mighty man who put forward the fantastic thesis that a horse's hoof could be bottomed like a saucepan—a pioneer with vision enough to dream a dream, and courage enough to persist in spite of the backward-pointing thumbs that were pointed at him out over shrugged shoulders. His name has not come down to us, but he was as big a man in his way as Columbus or Edison; and the quality that marked him out from his fellows was an imagination that glowed as brightly as the white metal he hammered and shaped.

CHILDREN'S PARTY

NOT every birthday means a party. If it did, parents would not last even as long as they do : there is a limit to what flesh and blood can stand. But if you let several birthdays go by without a party your children begin to regard you as a man without a conscience. They have been piling up debts in your name and they expect you to clear them off by giving a party. They are not really worried about the debts, of course : what they really want is to get more and more credit and to go to more and more parties.

At length a stage is reached when there is no hope of escape with honour. You have been cadging long enough, and you must stand your round. So you announce that you are going to give a party. And then you notice that one of your children has become suddenly popular. Little ladies whose hair she is in the habit of pulling keep the butts of their lollipops for her, her bitterest enemies knock at the door and ask " Will Nora be out ? " and everywhere she goes she is trailed by fawning sycophants.

When you hear her saying " Just for that you won't come to my party, Mabel Ryan ! " you realize that the whole thing is cut and dried. The date has still to be fixed (for parties are not always held on the birthday, nor even within the octave), but the hostess has already asked half the neighbourhood and is exacting tribute in advance from her guests. She is laden down with marbles,

coloured beads, " transfers ", comics, and girls' annuals.
She is living on the fat of the land. She may ride on
borrowed skates any time she feels like it, and she is
free to wheel out babies who at normal times are regarded as monopolies.

And these are only token payments, earnests of good
will, daily " sweeteners ". The best is yet to be, and
her battening has scarcely begun. For the really worth-
while perquisites are carried to the party in brown-paper
parcels and handed over with a mixture of pride and
regret by those who come to rejoice with the little hostess
on so happy an occasion, and incidentally to make beasts
of themselves with jelly and trifle and stoke up with
lemonade.

The real difficulty of a children's party is that of
keeping the guests amused during the intervals when
they are not eating. Little girls are easy enough, rela-
tively, for they are always willing to give recitations or
sing squeaky songs, but little boys expect something
more robust in the way of entertainment and usually
supply it themselves. And this can easily lead to prob-
lems of protocol. Thus you may have to reprimand
the host for telling one of the guests that he brought
" a rotten old present ", or intervene tactfully when a
visitor's nose is bleeding, and the host, who has obviously
bled it, explains with some heat that he was called " a
dirty eejit ". On occasions like these you must always
side against your own and suggest that the combatants
should shake hands and stand together for the singing
of " Holy Night ".

This may bring an uneasy peace but it won't bring any happiness, for communal singing at parties is not very popular with boys. It is not rowdy enough for them, and since it cuts down the time available for eating, they regard it as a miserly subterfuge that is not much above cheating. Late in the evening they may agree to sing such classics as " Rudolph the Red-Nosed Reindeer ", but they won't sing willingly until they are reasonably sure that all the food is finished and that the party is almost over—which in their view is much the same thing. At that stage they are ready to do almost anything. They will even play " Musical Chairs " or " Forfeits ", partly because they think that if they stick it out you will be forced to serve a final round of cake and lemonade, and partly because anything is better than going home.

This brings us to another difficulty of a children's party—how and when to finish it without sending for the police. Most adult parties finish of themselves and run down like spinning tops—sooner or later someone is bound to stand up and say " Isn't it about time we were thinking of going home, lads ? " and even though he may have to say it five or six times at widely spaced intervals, a sort of communal conscience will gradually awaken, and the host will be spared the shame of intimating that the festivities are drawing to a close. But there is no conscience, communal or otherwise, at a children's party. Both the inmates and the visitors are prepared to keep going indefinitely, and either the man or the woman of the house must make the first move.

So you say " Now we'll have a last song from Michael before we get the coats ", whereupon Michael sings

three songs, and he is followed by the shy boy in the
corner, who hasn't said a word all night but who now
decides to sacrifice himself and tell how Horatius kept
the bridge. An hour ago nobody wanted to sing, and
now everybody is bursting to sing. Nobody wants to
go home, and if you were to suggest a session of mental
arithmetic you would get enthusiastic support from the
most unlikely sources.

The parents who call to take their children home
should be a help, but often they aren't. They never
have time to come in, but they usually do come in.
They agree to sit down for a minute, and then stay an
hour drinking your sherry and doing conjuring tricks.
How long a children's party should last is a matter of
opinion, but you should always make an effort to get
the guests off the premises while you are still conscious.

In spite of all I have said I still think that a children's
party is a good investment, for it helps you to get rid
of your children : not for ever (that would be too much
to hope for) but on certain blessed evenings when other
parents will be paying off the debts incurred by their
offspring. All you have to do is to stake your own
children to a present a-piece and see that they wash
behind their ears. This done, you can put your feet
up. For an hour or two you are free of all responsibilities, and some unlucky neighbour will look after your
dear ones. Later on, you can visit the stricken house,
allow yourself to be coaxed in for a minute or two, and
drink a few glasses of sherry. And if you can waggle
your ears or do a few card tricks you will have no
difficulty at all in being the life and soul of the party.

SOFT DRINKS

THE only explanation I can offer for the labelling of drinks as " hard " or " soft " is that the whole thing was begun by hard drinkers, and that their object was not so much to label a kind of drink as to libel a kind of drinker. For your hard drinker is as careless with logic as with language. He renounces hard drinks from time to time, proclaims that he is " on the water wagon ", and then calls for a lemonade to prove that he is " on the dry ". This is the sort of thing that makes the language so difficult for foreigners.

The mental processes of the hard drinker are always involved and mysterious, but it is during his periodic bouts of virtue that he really reveals his complexity. He is not content with so negative a thing as abstention,

but must be the complete martyr. He even makes a
fuss of choosing his penance, dithering for a while
between lemon and orange—like an ascetic with a nice
taste in hair shirts—and finally settling for grape fruit.
And the reaction of a child to castor oil is not more
violent than the reaction of a great hulking man to
lemon soda or orange crush—the only outward difference
being that you have to prop the child's mouth open
and hold his nose.

But there is an important inward difference, for whilst
the child's revulsion is real and justified, the man's is
simulated and unjustified—as you can easily see by
refreshing your memory of the taste of castor oil and
weighing it against the taste of ginger pop. For the man
is not so much punishing himself as preening himself.
He wants you to think that he is drinking something
that tastes like a mixture of garlic and boot polish, and
of course he is doing nothing of the kind.

The soft drink, it must be admitted, has its limitations.
Lemonade drinkers, I have noticed, are not given to
throwing their hats over parapets, singing duets on the
tops of buses, or forcing cigars on newsboys; lemon
soda will not get a man into that mellow humour in
which he thinks that he is as good a man as the boss,
or into that still mellower humour in which he thinks
that he is as good a man as his wife; and orange crush
will not incite you to break tumblers for the fun of it
or swop vows of eternal friendship when you are parting
in the rain from fellows whom you will be meeting
again in the morning. But whilst the soft drink belongs
to the present and promises no dividends in the future,
there is one thing at least that can be said for it—it

tastes well. Taste is its only virtue, and it suffices : for it sells on its taste—unlike whiskey, gin, and brandy, which would still sell tolerably well if they were flavoured with lead paint, and which, like beer, caviare, stout, modern poetry, and chamber music, are acquired tastes.

Yet when a hardened drinker raises a soft drink to his lips he shudders and gives a passable imitation of a rigor. And then, doubling the libel, he closes his eyes—closes his eyes on a drink that glows with colour and movement, reflects the sun, and makes more commotion than champagne. Its " head " may not be as lasting as the head on a well-pulled pint of porter, but it has a finer texture—for the head on a pint of porter is no more pleasing, aesthetically, than a ploughman's shaving lather, and is as veined with rust as the great solid froth-fleeces that gather below waterfalls on mountain burns.

Children love lemonade. They love the fizz and sparkle of it, the cold, cutting taste of it, and the tickle that it gives the throat as it goes down. They can almost feel the beaded bubbles crumbling between their teeth. They tire in time of iced cake and trifle, and they sometimes leave a sliver of apple tart on the plate, but they would sell their nearest and dearest for lemonade, and the party is never over until the last siphon is empty.

It may seem that we outgrow our taste for lemonade, but I don't think that we do. What happens, rather, is that we grow ashamed of an early love when we hear it reviled by lugubrious fellows whose taste buds have been almost burnt away, and who, when they go on the dry, want the whole world to share their sorrow.

There is only one kind of drinking that is worse than solitary drinking—and that is sad drinking, especially when it goes with the heresy that by looking morose you lay up merit in heaven. It is understandable, I suppose, that great scrubby fellows should feel a little disconsolate when they give up strong drink temporarily, but soft drinks add nothing to their sorrow, and there is no reason why they should shake and tremble every time a little fruit juice and sugar—nicely laced with carbon dioxide—passes down their scarred and pitted gullets.

So far as I am concerned you may be wet or dry, hard or soft. You may drink what you please where you please, and perhaps we may have one together some day. But on one condition—you must look happy about it, whether you are taking gin-and-tonic, draught beer, Sauterne, or lemon crush, and especially if you are taking lemon crush. If you have abandoned strong drink for the good of body, or soul, or purse, I shall have every sympathy with you, but I shall give you no extra marks for drinking lemonade and looking glum about it. As things are, we have got into a nice tangle of logic and language, and there is no point in adding to the confusion by acting as if soft drinks were hard to take.

THE OLD CHEST

THESE sea-girt islands of ours have a climate that looks quite well in text-books and tourist brochures : but whilst the geographers describe it as temperate, the natives, who know it better, describe it as " bronical "; and with good reason, for they suffer for nine months out of the twelve, and for more in bad years (say, perhaps, two out of every three) from a complaint which gives endless food for discussion, advice, and prognosis, and is referred to, almost affectionately, as " the old chest ". The old chest is fatal, but in a benign and leisurely way. It gets us all in the end, but not before we are practically dead from something else, so that most of us manage to cough our way well into the seventies, whilst those who go sooner are regarded as having been cut off in the first flush of youth. And in the meantime, life is made very pleasant by immense quantities of hot punch.

Our chief indoor sport is coughing, which is also known as "clearing the old chest", and our best coughing is done in the early morning. We cough before we get up, we cough when we are getting up, and we cough to show that we *are* up : and each time we stop to draw breath we hear the man next door practising his arpeggios.

The morning cough, when heard at its richest, has two distinct notes : a heroic note, which tells a cold and heedless world that we are determined to struggle on; and a despairing note, which tells the rest of the household that we have not much time left for coughing, and that in a really Christian community we would be sent back to die in our beds. The morning cough, though basically involuntary, can be modified and prolonged at the will of the performer, and there are as many coughs as there are coughers. A cough is as distinctive as a signature, so that a trained ear can tell when there are strangers in church and recognize passers-by by their whinnies.

The street cough and the church cough, however, are marked by restraint, and it is only under his own roof that a man can really let himself go. The house cough has a solid base and a clearly-marked rhythm. It is built to a pattern, like a sonata, and it has a definite sequence of movements. A really good house cough, too, is not only vocal but articulate, so that it can express grumbles, maledictions, and fears of approaching dissolution. Indeed, in some of the remoter parts of the country, coughing largely replaces conversation from the first snowfall to the first crocus.

Among the commoner coughs heard in these temperate latitudes are the dog growl, the death rattle, the slow strangulation, and the " Another clean shirt will do me." But these are only rough classifications, for there are endless variations in tone, colour, and pitch, and no two coughs are alike. Some start like far-away thunder, and others are as sudden as a puncture; some finish cleanly on a sustained chord, and others die away in an arbitrary postscript of clocking-hen runs.

The real art of the morning cough is to give the impression that you are *in extremis* and that someone should go at once for the priest. It is bad technique to cough continuously, for this shows that you are still alive : you must always contrive spaced silences, during which the family can listen for the sound of your head striking against the edge of the bath. The feeling of crisis will be heightened if you moan from time to time and talk throatily to yourself. This will make it seem that you are struggling to make a verbal will and declaring with your last breath that Elizabeth is to get the piano.

Coughing in the bathroom is always very effective, as the acoustics are usually good there. If you cough until you shake like the harness on a hearse you are almost sure to be heard in the kitchen, and your wife will wonder if it worth while putting on your egg or not.

A good spell of bathroom coughing fits a man for the ordeal of shaving, and when he has made adequate comment on life and living he can draw his razor without flinching across the fleshy pockets under his chin. Bathroom coughing puts a man in fine fettle. It clears his head, eases the old chest, tones up the system, and gets the blood into circulation. He breathes deeply and draws cold air into his lungs. He might even burst into song, did he not know that in our climate it is dangerous to sing in the bathroom until you have left off your winter woollens. From the health point of view, coughing is as good as physical jerks, and much less tiring. Indeed it is one of the few forms of strenuous exercises that sedentary, bulging men are fit for before they get a poultice of porridge into them.

In the office, coughing should be done discreetly. You must cough enough to let the others know that you are a hero to come in at all, but continued paroxysms might lead to your being retired on a disability pension. Small seizures, however, will help you to gather your wits when you are asked awkward questions. They are also useful when you have to reprimand subordinates, and they give a knee-shaking quality to " I've had to speak to you before about your time-keeping, Smithers ", and " You are aware, I presume, that this is not a rest home."

Evening coughs should not be squandered, but should be conserved like ammunition. Timely bursts are advisable when there is any mention of bringing in coal for the fire or going to a whist drive, but they should not be over-done—you never know when one of the lads might ring up and ask you round for a game of Poker. It is well to brisk things up shortly before bedtime, however, lest your restraint should create an impression of vigorous health, and after a really convincing bout you should mutter brokenly that if you are to be fit for business in the morning you had better take something for the old chest.

All in all, our " bronical " climate has much to recommend it, and the fact that it tends to shorten life slightly rather than prolong it almost indefinitely is due solely to economic circumstances : or I might put it another way and say that the only thing that cuts down our supply of centenarians is the unconscionably high price of good whiskey.

CLOSE OF DAY

WAR drives men to strange employments. During the last war I dug trenches. Then I put manure into the trenches and laid sliced potatoes on top of the manure. In this way I produced a small quantity of food and came within an ace of leaving the country with one mouth less to feed. For the digging nearly killed me, and if I had gone the right way about it afterwards I might have got a pension.

But even the grimmest experience can be turned to good account, and although my bout with agriculture possibly shortened my life it brought me some enlargement of mind to set off against my varicose veins. I got on closer terms with wind and rain, I found what wireworms can do to potatoes, and I learned how to use a spade—thanks to the advice of a neighbour who saw that if I kept throwing each spit a foot into the air I wouldn't live to see the harvest.

Best of all, I got to know the man from Carndonagh and refreshed my knowledge of northern accent and idiom. He was thirty years out of Donegal, but he might never have left it, for I placed him to within thirty miles when I heard him speak.

I remember a thing he said to me one evening when we were the last to leave the field. (I was a great hand at leaning on a spade, and I used to ease my conscience sometimes by working into the gloaming.) His plot bordered mine—which suffered by the contrast, so that when you looked at the crops on them you were reminded of the Albert College experimental plots, and thought of "With superphosphate" and "Without superphosphate". But though I lost a little by being near him I gained far more than I lost. And I think that he gained something too, for I could speak his language: I was a northerner at one remove, and I knew the idiom of his mind.

We were both " earthing spuds " that evening, and once, when we met at the boundary, he straightened himself slowly until he stood black against the sunset. And then he said: " I think it's time to *lowse*." No one but myself, out of all the spatter of plotholders, would have known what he meant. It would have baffled Tourmakeady and set Macroom scratching his head. It would have meant nothing in Dingle or Thurles, but Doochary would have understood it at once and it would have been legal tender in the Rosses. What he meant was that it was time to unyoke—to " loose " the harness and call it a day. So I cleaned my spade on a bit of stone and took my stand beside him like a blood brother.

We unrolled our sleeves and got into our coats. He said nothing and I said nothing, but I knew that his thoughts matched mine, and I could see the picture in his mind. We were looking down on the city, but we were thinking of the Swilly and seeing a village at milking-time—a village with a single bumpy " street ", a village where the kitchen flagstones come out under the half-doors. And though the clamorous city beneath us was full of quietness, the village by the Swilly was full of sound.

The goslings, lately rounded up and shut away for the night, were chattering sleepily behind the slatted wooden gates of their stone houses. Fat pigs with soiled flanks and question-mark tails were being shepherded home, and gossiping dogs called from townland to townland. The rattle of the carts that were bringing back the last turf loads of the day could be heard from the shoulder of the mountain—a staggery, lurching rattle that might have been a furlong away instead of a mile, so that the ear made a liar of the eye. Heavy-uddered cows coming down from the high grazing parks stopped for a quick drink as they ankled through the little burn that the " druth " had dried up, and then went daintily-heavily up the lane. They padded round the corner of the house and into the darkness of the byre, and we heard the rattle of the chains about their creased, velvety necks as they mouthed hay in mangers and stood quietly for their milking.

There was a boy singing somewhere, and he stopped and started again continually—not at the end of a line or a phrase, but often in the very middle of a word. (Dear God, there is no singing like that nowadays, no singing of old songs with the dust of the years on them.) The corncrakes were crying the first watch of the night, and someone was playing a tin whistle down at the bridge—playing a naked tune, without harmonics or overtones, and going a little flat and screechy on the high notes, so that, as you listened, you had to stretch them a little and set the balance right. (There was a time when someone or other was always learning to play tin whistle or fiddle, and there was plenty of bad music everywhere. Now there is only the best, and the world has grown cold and joyless.)

Men coming from the fields with spades over their shoulders shouted greetings across half-doors as they lurched up the street, and stood on the lintels of byres to have a bit of crack with the women milking in the shadows. Everyone was busy, but no one hurried. The day was done, and it was ending slowly and quietly.

In the great cool kitchens, people were getting ready to debate the news of the day and discuss the year's prospects for spuds and corn. The men sat on the settle along the far wall, and the women crouched on stools near the heat. Turf fires burned red over their beards of white ash, and the porridge bubbled and spluttered under the heaving lids of the pots. (There is nothing like porridge, they used to say. Morning, noon, or night, it is a fine thing for the stomach. And it reared big strapping men who navvied their way round the world.)

. . . . .

I often think still of that day when myself and the man from Carndonagh walked home together in the heel of the evening and shared thoughts without speaking; and I think of it especially when I have a spade in my hand. (I have no love of spades, God knows, but the feel of a spade does a man good and reminds him that he has roots.) When it is time to *lowse*, when it is lamp-time and milking-time. I think of that great-hearted, incorruptible Donegal man who never really left home; and who, when he looked down on the lights of the city, saw instead the lights of a little village, and watched the night's dust sheets coming down on the hills across the wide, sea-going Lough.

HUMOUR AS I SEE IT

This essay should have come first, but my publisher put his foot down: and it wouldn't have come even last only I put my foot down. When he saw that I was obdurate he said " Well, provided that you put it far back." And I did. It couldn't be further back unless I put it among the end papers.

And even then he dithered a bit. (Remember all the trouble the Israelites had getting out of Egypt.) He asked me could I not make it funny, and then said " Well, er, you know."   This was an effort to save himself from the admission that he thought the rest of the book funny, which might have incited me to ask for a higher royalty.

(If you haven't ever met a publisher you have missed something.   A publisher is a man who, when he has two apples, eats one himself and keeps the other for the morning.)

I take this all back.   I am just trying to make a case for something which doesn't really belong to the book, but which I wanted in.   But I am not apologising.   Far from it.   I want to say this thing, and I think that it needs saying, but I just can't make it funny; though I may have made it fatuous—by getting out of my depth.

There is no need, however, for you to get out of yours. You can stop now if you want to.

I SEE humour as a flight; not as a flight from reality, but as a flight to reality.   When people laugh, they tell themselves that they want to get away from the things that matter, but what they really want to get away from are the things that don't matter. In order to live at all in this world of ours we have to make a compromise and adopt a false sense of values. We have to worry about mortgages, and tight shoes, and ill health. But once in a while we ease the tension by seeing our worries at their real, flea-bite size. We lift our minds then and see the joke, and the joke is that man is bigger far than anything that can happen to him. Humour and seriousness are complementary; they are opposite sides of the same pattern; and the funny story is not a digression from the sermon but part of the sermon.

Laughter, which is a characteristic human coefficient, gives the lie to materialism, for laughter is based on the incongruous, the foolish, the unexpected; and these things, to the thorough-going materialist, have no meaning except failure and tragedy. The basis of the materialist philosophy is that things must be brought to heel, that everything should be foreseen and planned for, and that the material thing called man can and must learn to dominate and control all the material things around him. If the tangible world about us is the only reality, if failure is real and for ever, and if the grave ends everything, then laughter is no more than spittle on the lips of fools.

A certain type of humour might be described as emotion recollected in tranquillity. When the fuss and the fret is over we sit down to laugh at our own foolishness, or at someone else's, and to-day's little tragedy becomes to-morrow's funny story. The psychologists and the philosophers have their own explanations

of this kind of laughter, but they are not very convincing.
The theologians might have done better, but the theologians have not spoken yet.   If they did speak they
might say something like this : " All manner of meaning-
less and insignificant things get the better of us here—
from leaking faucets to bunions—and laughter is an
attempt to get these tiny defects into proper perspective.
When we laugh we say ' I, the big thing, the immortal
thing, the rational thing, forgot my dignity and destiny
as a son of God and let a tiny thing rile me.' "   And
it may be that there will be quite a lot of this kind of
laughter in Heaven, when our sense of values will be
aligned with reality and geared for eternity.

Stephen Leacock says in *How to Write* that humour
may be defined as " the kindly contemplation of the
incongruities of life and the artistic expression thereof ".
But the thing that humour contemplates kindly is, not
the incongruities of life, but human nature itself.   The
kindly contemplation of a broken umbrella makes as
little sense as the kindly contemplation of a missing
collar-stud.   Human nature is not only the appraiser
but the source of incongruities : and there is no room
in the materialist philosophy for a kindly contemplation
of human nature; this can come only from pity, and
respect, and love, from a firm belief that God made us
and thought us worth the making, and that our present
poverty and exile will pass.

The incongruous thing, the anomalous thing, the
lovable thing, is that wildest of paradoxes, man himself.
He is less than the dust, but greater than the sun.   The
tiniest virus can kill him, but he will live for ever.   He
is lower than the angels, but his Mother is the Queen

of Angels. Badgered and baffled, he remains invulner-
able. The dogs may lick his sores, but his destination
is Abraham's bosom. All the best humour of life derives
from this sorry and glorious two-legged joke: and all
the thoughts that are worth thinking stem from it.

There is nothing funny about stupidity. What is
funny is that we were not meant to be stupid. We were
meant to be lords of the earth. Man, in short, is not
the man he used to be—not since Adam; and he is
certainly not the man God meant him to be. He has
been shorn and circumscribed. His wings have been
clipped. And because of an incident that is known
as the Fall, the terms of his contract have been
drastically revised. A lot of people no longer believe
in the Fall, but it is a very comforting doctrine.
It helps you to laugh at foolishness, even at your own
foolishness; it teaches you that you are God's fool.

The story of the Fall is that God made man and gave
him the earth for a garden. Then man rebelled and
lost his tenancy, and a wild disharmony arose both
within and without. Weeds, and termites, and locusts
became his enemies; wind and sun joined in the conspiracy; and man had to fight his corner with a weakened
will and a darkened intellect.

But he was not one whit abashed. He cudgelled his
tiny brain and proved that God is not. He made golden
calves and worshipped them. He blasphemed and cried
for mercy, he built temples to unchaste goddesses. And
God looked down on it all.

God looked down on it all, and held His hand, because
His justice is tempered with mercy, and because in His

feelings for us there is pity, and tenderness, and love.
And the thing that He loves most in us, perhaps, is
our littleness.

Yet out littleness is not for ever. What is for ever
is our bigness—for nothing but bigness can last as long
as that. And it may well be that all humour is a mirror
of this tremendous incongruity, that we make little jokes
now because we have only a faint and shadowy grasp
of the greatest joke of all, and that our first slice of
eternity will be spent in rationalizing this thing that we
call a sense of humour, and in seeing ourselves for the
first time in our proper size.